Pick of the Bunch

NEW ZEALAND *W*ILDFLOWERS

PETER JOHNSON

Longacre Press

By the same author:

WILDFLOWERS OF CENTRAL OTAGO
1986

WETLAND PLANTS IN NEW ZEALAND
(with Pat Brooke, 1989)

FLOWERING PLANTS OF NEW ZEALAND
(Colin Webb, Peter Johnson, & Bill Sykes, 1990)

ISBN 1 877135 06 2

First published 1997 by Longacre Press Ltd.,
P.O. Box 5340, Dunedin, New Zealand.

Cover and book design by Jenny Cooper
Map by Ana Terry
Electronic pre-press by Hughes Lithographics, Dunedin
Printed by Tablet Colour Print, Dunedin

DEDICATION

In memory of Tim Johnson, 1973–1996,
who loved the challenge of places wild
and high, and the contemplation of
beauty, truth, and existence.

ACKNOWLEDGEMENTS

Thank you Pru, for sharing holidays with a wildflower theme and
so many photographic interruptions, and for giving the book its title.
Thank you Peter Williams, Carol West, and Colin Webb,
botanical friends, for commenting on the manuscript,
and Brian Turner for editorial suggestions.

Down by a riverside

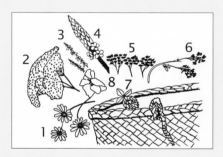

1. Scentless mayweed,
   Tripleurospermum inodorum
2. Wild carrot, *Daucus carota*
3. White melilot, *Melilotus albus*
4. Woolly mullein, *Verbascum thapsus*
5. Yarrow, *Achillea millefolium*
6. Lucerne, *Medicago sativa*
7. Red clover, *Trifolium pratense*
8. Sand primrose, *Oenothera stricta*

It was a dry summer morning and we were on the road out of Hastings. Somewhere west of Waipukurau our attention was caught by the many colours of lucerne flowers, purple through to white. We pulled in to a gravel pit beside the Makaretu River and filled a kete with lucerne and other wildflowers of roadside and riverside. This was the first of many bunches of flowers put together for a group photograph. They are all flowers we shall meet again, as we travel round the country.

Contents

1 Introduction

Here is my pick of pictures and a bunch of stories about New Zealand wildflowers.

In different parts of the world the term wildflower has strong associations with field or forest, heathland or hedgerow, marsh or mountainside. New Zealand has all these habitats, and more. Despite its modest size, our country provides diverse landforms, climates, and soils for distinct assemblages of flowering plants.

To my way of thinking, wild-flowers are unassisted wayside plants, colourful either in a literal sense or because they have some story to tell. For this definition I have been called a cock-eyed optimist. Undismayed, I extend the optimism in this book to a mixed selection from the approximately 2,100 native flowering plants and the 1,800 or so species that have become naturalised here from overseas. Furthermore, to really stretch my definition, I have thrown in the odd wild fruit, a fern or two, and even a fungus. Overall I have attempted to give a nationwide coverage of the more obvious and accessible wildflowers. In addition, many of the less common gems have been included from tucked-away corners of Aotearoa.

Some degree of "pickability" comes into my concept of wildflowers, though not necessarily the classic tidy posy that would be gathered by the young woman with the long dress and the flowing hair in one of those slow motion, frosted lens, fuzzy margin, advertising shots. More in mind is the she'll-be-right equivalent – a ragged little fistful of flowers plucked for Mum by one of the kids; or the not-quite-ikebana bunch, loosely splayed in a glass jar or jammed into a milk bottle to decorate the hut table or holiday window-sill; or the little treasures of flora deposited on the

Flower buds of sweet brier *(Rosa rubiginosa)* gift-wrapped by a nurseryweb spider *(Dolomedes minor).*

car dashboard where they will add their withered petals to the inner workings of the demist system.

"What if everybody picked the wildflowers?", the cautious punters might ask, "and what would be the impacts?" I hesitate to offer many guidelines for picking flowers. Clearly there are places where native vegetation has legal protection, or where lots of people congregate and might take too many flowers, or situations where the flowers have been planted yet not for picking. But if flowers are abundantly present, then picking a small proportion is unlikely to have much impact on the reproductive success of the plants. The bunches of flowers in this book were picked from populations where their collection was judged to have minimal impact.

My stories are arranged as a journey, starting in southern New Zealand, heading to the far north, then coming more-or-less back home, by a different route. Really it is an amalgam of journeys, that are composite in time and zigzag in direction. On the way we may become distracted or temporarily lost among the odd detail or generality, and experience those uninvited feelings or unexpected enlightenments which appear on any trip, and which, for me, have linkages with particular people and places and plants.

Our starting place on the map is a bulge of land jutting into the world's biggest ocean, just a degree closer to the South Pole than to the Equator: a peninsula of grassy hills and scattered remnants of native bush, of unfrequented beaches and sea-cliffs, and having wildflowers of one sort or another. We start here, on Otago Peninsula, because this is the familiar territory of home, centre of my universe, reference point for all my explorations. *Let's go…*

Beyond the back lawn

1. Bracken, *Pteridium esculentum*
2. Yorkshire fog, *Holcus lanatus*
3. Lotus, *Lotus pedunculatus*
4. White clover, *Trifolium repens*
5. Sheep's sorrel, *Rumex acetosella*

You wouldn't need to wander far from any New Zealand backyard to come across one or more of this lot. Weeds all of them, some of the time, but not always. Where would our cockies rest without clover? What better than lotus for hydro-seeding a new road-cutting? Sheep's sorrel is an abundant weed, with yellow rhizomes to help the gardener trace the scoundrel underground, and masses of tiny flowers which can turn stony uplands red. The arrow-shaped leaves have been known to poison livestock, yet are sometimes included in salads for their sharply acidic taste. Presumably sheep get some tucker-value out of sheep's sorrel, though they probably much prefer the softly hairy grass, Yorkshire fog.

Of all the above plants, bracken fern is the one that has been useful to people in this land for the longest. For many centuries before the high-fibre diet was in fashion, the starchy rhizomes, aruhe, gave the old people something to chew on.

2 *Close to Home*

My world is a garden. It starts at the back door, in a relatively tamed and tidy state, with manageable domesticated trees and flowers, but near the boundary hedges we start to meet their real wild cousins.

Daphne laureola might be regarded as a shady character. A low shrub with dark leaves, it turns up under hedges, shrubberies and plantations. The greenish-yellow flowers are almost clandestine in their modesty and save their release of fragrance till after dusk.

Daphne laureola growing wild beneath our back hedge.

A markedly less shy and more demonstrative plant grows out on our roadside bank. Giant bugloss is a real boom-and-bust plant, being a hoary, large-leaved herb in its first year, then producing a woody trunk-like stalk and a smothering of blue flowers, before seeding and dying within its second year. Giant bugloss originates from the Canary Islands off the north-west Africa coast, and is a relative newcomer to the New Zealand scene, found from Kaikohe to Stewart Island, especially on rubbly coastal banks near settlements.

Most of the wildflowers readily seen in New Zealand are plants that have become established here only within the last 150 years. For thousands and millions of preceding years the natural wildflowers near our home would have been those of the native forest that grew here. Sometimes it crosses my mind that the place where I sleep, upstairs, every night, is a space that should properly belong to the limbs and flowers of kowhai trees.

As we climb the hill behind home a theme recurs of old plants mixed with new, survivors alongside invaders, on land littered with symbols of its genesis and history. Beyond the macrocarpas of our back boundary, we pass first through a buttercup paddock, created by the selective gourmet grazing of horses which have chewed the grasses and spurned the less palatable buttercups. The next paddock has a spur of pasture where the native ti, or cabbage tree, once added its blossom sweetness to the air. Although none grow there now, dimpled ground and occasional red-baked rocks reveal the sites of earth

Giant bugloss, *Echium pininana*, its blue flowers mostly finished, showing off its unique flower stalks (to 5.6 m tall). Otago Harbour beyond.

Kowhai, *Sophora microphylla*, Otago Peninsula.

ovens, umu-ti, where the starchy ti trunks and rootstocks were roasted to sweet fructose by the Ngai Tahu Confectionery Company.

There is evidence of kowhai trees having also once been common. Kowhai wood shows its characteristic herringbone pattern on the end grain of many of the early fenceposts. But some kowhai trees persist in the bush-remnant gully, having escaped the axe and the matchbox, and beginning about August every year they turn on a golden display and a welcome spring nectar source for the birds. Come November and it is the turn of the weedy hawthorn trees to go overboard with their carnival of blossoms and their heady scent. About this time of year we cross a little hill to catch the peak flowering of foxgloves, purple and white, among the kanuka and cow-pats at the Glen, or else take a longer walk across the peninsula.

Ah… how different the outer coast is. In just an hour and a half's walk we are standing on 200 m sea-cliffs carved out of old lava flows by the swell and fury of the South Pacific. This is an awful place on south-west storm days, and a miserable penetrating damp place on north-east drizzle days, but on the fine mornings of the growing season the flowers here are warmed by the sun for many hours before we get out of bed. On the rock ribs of the cliffs we find the most local yokel of native plants, a form of the whipcord daisy shrub, *Helichrysum intermedium* previously known by the name *H. selago* var. *tumidum*, and confined to just two Otago coastal headlands. Beside it, crusting the rocks, is the snowpake lichen, and on the ledges with deeper soil are the flags of the flax plant.

Foxgloves, *Digitalis purpurea*, up the Glen, Otago Peninsula. This is a bicultural bit of vegetation (as opposed to a mono-culture), with just two main plants: a second-growth forest of old kanuka, *Kunzea ericoides*, and an understorey of foxgloves.

Harakeke, New Zealand flax, *Phormium tenax*; and whipcord daisy, *Helichrysum intermedium*, on the high sea-cliffs of Sandymount, Otago Peninsula.

3 *Flying the Flag*

From time to time suggestions are made to change the New Zealand flag, away from the hotchpotch of stars, blue sky, and the criss-cross of pickets, red and white, that represent the fighting shields carried by the Saints of Scotland, England, and Ireland. We fly a banner that is barely different from the Australian one, and neither nation seems willing to shed its twinset of baby garb. No national koru flag seems likely to be unfurled for a while yet.

An idea that appeals to me, from Graeme Platt, native plant enthusiast of Albany, is that New Zealand flax should be the basis of our flag. The flax genus, *Phormium*, has been gifted almost exclusively to New Zealand. With its distinctive, almost stylised shape, it seems already pre-disposed for use as a symbol of pride and nationalism. What is more, you could make an excellent hard-wearing cloth flag from the fibres of the same plant.

Flowers of harakeke, *Phormium tenax*, Otago Peninsula.

Flax is a plant which flies its own flag. It has tall flagpoles on which the flowers and later the fruits are flown, and it is flying creatures – birds and insects – which visit the flagpoles. The likes of tuis and bellbirds come to do pollinating service and to lap up the nectar. If for some reason you cut and pick a stout stem of flax in full flower and carry it under your arm, over your shoulder, or any way other than upright, you will discover just how much weight and volume of sticky nectar is poised in the bucket end of the flowers.

Phormium is restricted to New Zealand, except that *P. tenax* gets to Norfolk Island. There are only two species, this one and *P. cookianum*, but numerous races and cultivars of both. I love our flaxes for their variability, the different flower colours, the curly tipped pods, the flaky seeds, shiny coal black. Come to think of it, I have seen flax turned to coal, the overlapping leaves recognisable as an etched thatch on a coal mine ceiling.

The so-called mountain flax, wharariki, *Phormium cookianum*. This plant, growing on the Nelson coast at Totaranui, has the yellow or green outer tepals (and flaccid leaves, not shown) of the northern lowland form, *P. cookianum* subsp. *hookeri*.

Opposite page:
Flax on the shore of Kapiti Island, off the Wellington coast. Erect seed pods tell us that this is *Phormium tenax*. (The other species, *Phormium cookianum*, has hanging, twisted pods.)

Flax – harakeke – has been here millions of years; it belongs to a tangata whenua of extremely long standing. It is still standing strong, and is a plant for which I would say a lot of New Zealanders feel a marked level of respect. Many people grow it and many must use it. An unseen strip of flax has been used to tie or support some of the bunches of flowers in this book. The kete on page 6 is made of it: *Phormium*, the basket plant, having *tenax*, tenacity. We have on Otago Peninsula, a Harakeke Point, a high headland with plenty of flax on the hill crest above the sea-cliffs. It is an ideal place for hurling flax darts because the best ones will hold their height on the updraught for some time, then stall and dive-bomb like gannets into the sea. Adjacent to Harakeke Point, a huge expanse of dune sand has blown 300 metres up to the hill crest of Sandymount, once a place where flax was grown and milled for the good fibre, and once also, a target site for dive-bombing practice by the air force. Bits of bomb used to turn up in the sand. The flying log-book of my father records that he was doing dry dives in that area, in a Mustang, just six days before his final flight. I remember. Once we walked, he and I, among harakeke.

If you have good reason to attack a flax bush with a pocket knife (garden pruning perhaps, or clearing a track to the maimai), you get an opportunity to see the colours and beautiful sheathing overlaps of the leaf bases, and the cross-sections of the fibrous veins, and the clear jelly which the harakeke plant exudes to protect and waterproof, heal and varnish itself.

The delicate petals of native linen flax, *Linum monogynum*, can be pale blue instead of white. This rocky cliff plant, photographed on the Otago Peninsula coast, is not to be confused with the New Zealand flax genus *Phormium*. It is related instead to the northern hemisphere *Linum usitatissimum*, sometimes found wild in New Zealand, and cultivated for flax fibre and linseed oil.

The Flax from Hackett River

Making a bunch of these plants in different parts of New Zealand would seldom produce an identical result, for all three species display much variation in plant size, leaf shape and flower colour. Shown here are a typical mountain flax with red outer tepals and green inner ones; a rather frilly-flowered kanuka; and a red-eyed form of manuka. They are all tough sorts of plants too, found in many extreme habitats. This assemblage was growing in stunted scrub up the Hackett River near Nelson, on the so-called mineral belt of reddish ultramafic rocks where the soils are starved of some nutrients, yet often toxic with high concentrations of heavy metals.

1. Mountain flax, wharariki, *Phormium cookianum.*
2. Kanuka, *Kunzea ericoides.*
3. Manuka, *Leptospermum scoparium.*

4 Around the Bay Road

I wonder how many parts of the country have a "bay road" as part of the local geography, to juxtapose somewhere among the Black Peaks, Cattle Flats, and Muddy Creeks. We have a "high road" along the crest of the hills and a "bay road" along the edge of Otago Harbour, although neither colloquial name appears on the maps. The "bay road" – basically a winding cart track that has been tar-sealed – is flanked on the harbour side by a beautifully built sea-wall of hand-placed rock, and on the landward side by a towering bank, bedecked with flowers at every season.

Giant aeonium, *Aeonium undulatum*, Otago Harbour.

This is a very favourable home for many wild flowering plants. The rubbly banks are unstable yet fertile, perfectly drained, virtually frost-free, well-lit and well-warmed, and they score the bonus of extra energy reflected off the harbour waters, especially by the low-angled rays of winter sun.

The road bank is ornamented with wallflowers, said to have been planted by the people who once ran the toll-gate on the road. There are cresses like alyssum and stocks, succulents like giant aeonium which shows off so nicely its spirals of leaf and flower arrangement, wild herbs like parsley, and the wild vegetables, parsnip and cabbage. The cabbages are heartless things that have lost their breeding and culinary appeal. Nevertheless, they put on a fine display of pale yellow flowers; and when a botanist from the United States requested old cabbage cultivars for his studies on genetic variation within this most important and varied of vegetable and fodder plants, the seeds of these Otago Harbour plants were exactly the sort of thing he wanted.

What else? ... at least another hundred wildflowers and weeds, as well as plants that have escaped from cultivation or been discarded by gardeners. Many of them are Mediterranean plants, and a similar assemblage of species turns up together round other harbours further north: Lyttelton, Wellington, and Napier, for example.

From the window at the top of our stairs I can look across the harbour and catch sight of the ships which enter Port Chalmers to load containers, logs, or woodchips. They berth beneath the cliffs of Flagstaff Hill, which in early summer are dusted white with marguerite daisy, and yellow with the shrubby stonecrop. Once, I had the job of advising on a revegetation scheme for this cliff garden, for replanting

after quarrying had removed more of the headland for port expansion. That was an interesting and unusual exercise in garden design, but an equally memorable association with Flagstaff Hill was the day of my visit to take the stonecrop photo. Crockery dinner plates were being chucked out from a clifftop dwelling, accompanied by shouts. Believing myself out of sight, I concluded they were not being thrown at me. Was I instead a witness to some domestic dispute, to an expression of artistic temperament, or to an act of defiance towards the Port Company?

Shrubby stonecrop, *Sedum praealtum*, at Port Chalmers, Otago Harbour.

Pride of Madeira, *Echium candicans*, at Macandrew Bay, Otago Harbour. This photo was taken before Kerry McKay decorated the boatshed. Nowadays a permanent line of ducks flies across the wall, mermaids are painted either side of the front door, and there is a carved hand which pulls a blind over the front window.

Wild cabbage, *Brassica oleracea*, on the Otago Harbour sea-wall.

Opposite page:
Australian ice plant,
Disphyma clavellatum,
beside Otago Harbour.

Purple succulents

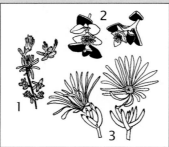

1. *Drosanthemum floribundum.*
2. *Aptenia cordifolia.*
3. *Lampranthus spectabilis.*

Succulent plants have leaves or stems that are thickened, soft, and watery, an adaptation to dry or salty climates. These three examples have several things in common. They are South African plants, with a few springbok genes perhaps, for they have all leaped out of New Zealand gardens to grow wild on coastal rocks and banks. All belong to the same family (Aizoaceae), and despite being placed in three different genera, they are identical in flower colour. I have seen this colour referred to as "cyclamen-cerise". They grow wild together on roadside banks beside Otago Harbour.

Ice plants from many lands

Ice plants are named for the frosted, glistening, crystalline tissues seen when a turgid leaf is snapped in two. What a satisfying clean snap it makes! These are all coastal plants which grow as fleshy carpets or even as curtains from above a rock overhang. The imported ice plants are usually found half-wild where they have been planted on sand-dunes and banks, close to harbours and coastal towns. Native ice plant is found all along our coasts, on cliff ledges and rubble slopes.

You may wonder why the name pig face has been bestowed on the largest of these ice plants. The answer comes when you recognise the piglets which become apparent upon the ripening fruit, after the flowers are spent. The fleshy leaves and sepals curve around to give them snouts, ears, and tusks. Carpobrotus leaves are sharply triangular in cross-section. Pig face (C. edulis) has yellow flowers which turn to pinkish-orange as they grow older, so that the plant often exhibits both flower colours. Ice plant (C. aequilaterus) can be distinguished by its purple petals, paler at the base.

Disphyma *leaves are shorter and less sharply three-angled than those of* Carpobrotus. *In native ice plant (D. australe), flower colour ranges from white to deep pink. The Australian* D. clavellatum, *known from near Invercargill and Dunedin, has smaller purple flowers, 2-4 cm across, and fat blunt-tipped leaves.*

The hybrid ice plant is interesting for it involves one New Zealand parent and one South African. A hybrid between two genera is unusual, though it is often an indication of taxonomic closeness of the two. This hybrid is infertile and does not reproduce itself by seed. One test for identifying hybrid ice plant is to dab a moist finger onto the ring of anthers in the centre of the flower and reveal that the sterile flowers have not managed to produce any yellow grains of pollen.

1. Pig face, *Carpobrotus edulis*, from South Africa.
2. Ice plant, *Carpobrotus aequilaterus*, from California and Chile.
3. Hybrid ice plant, *Carpobrotus edulis* ✕*Disphyma australe*.
4. Native ice plant, *Disphyma australe*, endemic to New Zealand.
5. Australian ice plant, *Disphyma clavellatum*, from Australia.

5 Spring in the Air

Winter heliotrope,
Petasites fragrans,
Dunedin.

Winter heliotrope,
Petasites fragrans,
Dunedin.

What a great time of year spring is. The time when new life bursts forth. Sap rises and seedlings spring up. Bleating newborn lambs appear in the paddocks. Spring is supposed to be the season for romance and sex, for shows of blossom and pretty flowers, and all these things associated one with another. To someone from a non-temperate climate all this must seem a little strange.

In New Zealand spring is not a great snow-melt event. In that third or so of the country which might be regarded as mountainous, snow is forever falling and melting, and it is hard to say which melt event actually heralds spring, whether it is the warm rain which denudes such-and-such a ski-field, or the general warming that turns the mountains into such an avalanche danger about October and November.

Wallflower,
*Cheiranthus
cheiri*, on
coastal cliffs
at Long Beach,
near Dunedin.

Spring is cumulative. Summer is a whole set of expectations, myths, pleasures or disappointments: there can be no last word about summer. Autumn is degenerative. Winter is persistent.

Winter heliotrope, an invasive old garden plant of rough urban roadsides, bears its sweet-smelling flowers between June and September. This strategy of flowering very early in spring may enable winter heliotrope to get in first, before there is much competition for insect pollinators. Whereas both sexes must be present in its native North Africa, the introduced plants in both Europe and New Zealand are all males, chaste and isolated.

Wallflower is another indication of early spring with its yellow, brown or reddish flowers. How I love the unusual rich brown flowers of some individuals, and a good whiff of the smell of all of them. I chose Long Beach, north of Dunedin, as the place to photograph wallflowers, because the sea-cliffs here are an old favourite rock-climbing crag, and I have many memories of sharing a toe-hold or a belay point with a wallflower, and with glistening crystals of olivine and hornblende on a sun-warmed face of volcanic rock.

Right: Snowflake, *Leucojum aestivum*, is a spring bulb which persists within old farm gardens. This old weatherboard villa, and somebody's former garden, are beside the Karamea River, North Westland, but they could equally well be at several other remote corners of pioneer New Zealand.

Two spring bulbs which gardeners sometimes confuse are the snowdrop (*Galanthus*) and the taller and more leafy snowflake (*Leucojum*). The snowflake is more likely to be found semi-wild. Both this and the daffodil can actually increase after sheep and cattle gain access to an abandoned farm garden, an example of the success that comes from a chemical investment in unpalatability. The leaves of snowflake are described as lorate, meaning strap-shaped, and while they are apt to flop about, the flower stalk is stiffened by two or three gently spiralling flanges, which share this strengthening feature with angle iron.

In the weedy and unpleasant-smelling onion weed (*Allium triquetrum*), the white flowers are held on a stalk that is triangular in cross-section, a feature that has given rise both to the species name *triquetrum* and to one of its common names, three-cornered garlic. The real garlic and the real onion are different species of *Allium*.

Sufferers of hay fever find spring and summer the most trying of seasons. Pollen is a frequent trigger for many allergies, especially the pollen from grass flowers. "Why grass pollen?" the sufferer may ask, "and anyway, where are the flowers on grasses?". It comes as a surprise to many people to discover that grasses do have flowers, even though they lack size and have no showy petals. Rather than trying to be attractive to insect or bird pollinators, their method for achieving pollen transfer from one flower to another or from one plant to another is to rely instead on the wind.

In the photo of the cocksfoot flower head we see masses of purple anthers, each one finely suspended at the end of a white filament. Fine jiggling by even the slightest breeze releases the yellow pollen, a fraction of which will be wafted to catch upon the feathery stigmas – the female receptors – of other flowers.

To overcome the inefficiency of this strategy, grasses must produce vast numbers of lightweight pollen grains – hence the contribution to runny noses and the seasonal timing of TV and newspaper ads for anti-histamine treatments: spring in the air indeed.

Onion weed, *Allium triquetrum,* in the Dunedin Town Belt.

The tiny grass flowers of cocksfoot, *Dactylis glomerata,* hanging their purple stamens out for the breeze.

A bunch for September

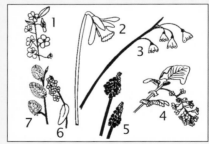

From a flowering point of view, spring is not one event, but a whole sequence of awakenings over several months. This is an early September selection from Dunedin: all of them being plants that have spread from gardens.

1. Plum, *Prunus ×domestica*.
2. Daffodil, *Narcissus pseudonarcissus*.
3. Snowflake, *Leucojum aestivum*.
4. Flowering currant, *Ribes sanguineum*.
5. Grape hyacinth (match heads), *Muscari armeniacum*.
6. Forget-me-not, *Myosotis sylvatica*.
7. Pussy willow, *Salix ×reichardtii*.

6 It's All Right Here

Whereas many American movies counteract their peaks of panic with the glib hope that "everything's gonna be alright", Dunedin city has adopted the line "It's all *right* here". By this slogan visitors are lured and residents reassured, especially when Rhododendron Week takes on an authentic Himalayan foothill feel by copping a few days of cold, wet southerlies.

Along with a select few other parts of the country (Bay of Plenty, and Westland), Dunedin can boast *Rhododendron ponticum* among its wildflowers, growing with wild primroses by the hilltop reservoir that serves Port Chalmers. This *Rhododendron* was one of the earliest species introduced into cultivation in Europe and again in New Zealand. It is now becoming a problem weed in the woods and moorlands of the British Isles, so we should be wary of letting it get out of hand in our southern isles.

Rhododendron ponticum beside the reservoir on Mihiwaka Hill near Dunedin.

Another famous feature of Dunedin is its main stream, quaintly named the "Water of Leith", famed (or forgotten) as the first liberation site for trout in New Zealand. Today the concrete-walled lower channel of the Leith may not look much like a trout stream, but as kids we found it well-stocked with tiddlers, hungry for a worm on a hook, and the odd one- or two-pounder. There were other catches too. An enterprising Chinese boy in our scout group knew where and how to catch enough whitebait to feed his family. Our envy was tempered by the knowledge that the Leith was not super-clean; the memorable and truly disgusting catch by my brother David of a sack of dead cats was a fish story that my mother never wanted to hear at the dinner table.

In flood, the Water of Leith is the channel by which the junk of student flats is sent downstream to the harbour: cardboard cartons, clapped-out couches, crippled supermarket trollies, and dead telly sets. Coming upstream, in the face of flood and flotsam are huge spawning trout and salmon that leap the falls to the fascination of children and professors alike. Provided these sea-run fish avoid being poached and fried by students, relocated by the Fish and Game Council, or back-stabbed by a black shag, they will travel upstream, past the university where the Mexican daisy and the 'Alberic Barbier' roses grow on the concrete walls above the stream, to the mother gravel

Winter cress, *Barbarea intermedia*, Leith Valley, Dunedin.

beds where the next generation of fingerlings will start life, beside the watercress beds of summer.

Winter cress and honesty are just two of the colourful annual weeds that colonise the stream gravels between floods. The name honesty presumably alludes to the transparent fruits. The generic name *Lunaria* refers to the lunar shapes of the seeding capsules. When the fruits are ripe the side valves can be peeled off to leave a silvery septum, used in dried floral arrangements (see p. 169).

One of the nice things about Dunedin, and the valley of the Leith in particular, is that you can reach untamed bush country in just a few minutes drive from the city. A couple of weedy shrubs add their colour to the road and forest margins. Flowering currant performs in spring; it is found as a weed in many cooler parts of the country. Like many rhododendrons, and as its name suggests, Himalayan honeysuckle comes from somewhere near the world's highest mountains. In New Zealand this pretty shrub has become a weed, often colonising cutover bush. The white tubular flowers of Himalayan honeysuckle would be inconspicuous were it not for the pendulous pagoda in which they are displayed, among tiers of red-purple bracts.

Mexican daisy, *Erigeron karvinskianus*, in the tiny crevices of the concrete channel of the Water of Leith, as it passes the University of Otago.

Honesty, *Lunaria annua*, Leith Valley.

Flowering currant, *Ribes sanguineum*, beside the Leith Valley road.

Himalayan honeysuckle, *Leycesteria formosa*, at Trotters Gorge, near Dunedin.

Above:
The ripening fruits of honesty, with a backlit "x-ray" view of the seeds inside.

7 *A Daisy a Day*

Combining native with naturalised daisy species (over 500 in total), gives more than enough for a different daisy a day over the whole year.

The name daisy comes from day's eye – the sun or matahari – represented in the often yellow disc of a typical daisy flower head. A daisy head, although resembling a single flower, is actually made of many tiny flowers. Typically those in the outermost row each contribute one petal-like structure, termed a ray: another sunshine analogy.

From time to time I am approached by film agencies making TV commercials for the European market and seeking some made-to-order natural film set, say a landscape of white daisies, or a field of yellow ones. The scene with the yellow daisies, somewhere between Otorohanga and Kawhia, is one of the vague localities I have sent them. Has this scene ever appeared on French or German television, I wonder, and to advertise what?

Yellow daisies, mainly catsear, *Hypochoeris radicata*, near Otorohanga.

Chicory, *Cichorium intybus*, at Te Kuiti. The flowers are an incomparable pale sky blue. The processed rootstock is used as a substitute for, or an additive to, processed coffee.

Dandelion, *Taraxacum officinale*, from a weedy back corner of our Dunedin garden.

Coltsfoot, *Tussilago farfara*, from inland Canterbury. Coltsfoot is one of those youthful invaders poised to become a more widespread weed, especially in wet gravels.

Ragwort, *Senecio jacobaea*, near Wellsford.

Marigold, *Calendula officinalis*, between the coast road and the rubbish tip, Kakanui. *Calendula* is so-named because it can be found in flower during all calendar months of the year.

Bone-seed, *Chrysanthemoides monilifera*, beside Otago Harbour. Most other daisies have a brittle seed on a fluffy parachute. This one has a fleshy fruit, with a hard stony seed, hence the common name.

Stinking mayweed, *Anthemis cotula*, on the flood terrace of the Piako River, near Thames.

Six common daisies

1. Oxeye daisy, *Leucanthemum vulgare.*
2. Fireweed, *Senecio minimus.*
3. Ragwort, *Senecio jacobaea.*
4. Yarrow, *Achillea millefolium.*
5. Hawksbeard, *Crepis capillaris.*
6. Catsear, *Hypochoeris radicata.*

Presumably the oxeye daisy has the eyelashes of an ox, but has anybody seen a cow or a cattle-beast with a yellow-centred eye. Maybe many dairy cows have a jaundiced view of the economy. To link the name catsear to a cat you need to look at the leaves, while the beard of the hawksbeard adorns the fluffy air-borne seeds.

Fireweed doesn't have much of a show of flowers, less than its introduced cousin the ragwort. Fireweed is the only native plant in this bunch, and not one I would recommend for native plant gardeners. It turns up as a garden weed, uninvited, and is one of a group of Senecio species which appear in masses after a bush burn.

The yarrow we've seen before and we'll see again on more roadsides. The daisies in this bunch were picked from rough bush-edge pasture near Dunedin, from between Mopanui and Mihiwaka, a pair of hills with singing names, dancing skylines, part of my everyday view to the north.

8 Heading North

Dunedin to Christchurch by road takes four to five hours at the legal speed. Fairly typical highway: two lanes, an occasional road works gang, a littering of truck tyre fragments and bits of dried magpie, both in ragged curls. Mostly the road is straight and the landscape flat, with mere traces of whatever native greenery once grew here. Instead it has...

> From Oamaru to Timaru,
>   *Trifolium* and *Lolium*
>   stretched out like green linoleum.

Trifolium repens is white clover and *Lolium perenne* is perennial ryegrass. Together these two plants feed a lot of livestock, export markets, and mouths overseas. It is said that white clover is worth billions of dollars to New Zealand.

Always, one's first experience comes to mind as a reference point, so for this road journey I cast my mind back to the age of five, travelling with my parents in a massive old square box of a car called a Hudson Terraplane, a solid survivor of the days when cars had running boards like doorsteps along each side. It was winter. There was no heater. The comfort of the boy in the back seat was helped by a hotty, refilled somewhere along the way.

Gorse afire: how we manage to perpetuate *Ulex europaeus*; Weatherston Hill near Dunedin.

Boredom and confinement were relieved by, for example, "...counted all the bridges. There were some long ones. It was dark when we got to Christchurch and I went straight to bed. We got there IN TIME." (My diary, dictated, 18.5.1952.) At that age I had a slightly fearful regard for this concept called time. This supposedly ongoing dimension which nevertheless seemed to underly those adult concerns about urgency, punctuality, deadlines. Was time about to run out? Was the whole concept trustworthy, reliable?

Fennel, *Foeniculum vulgare*, by the old Green Island Railway Station, near Dunedin. This tall feathery herb with the aniseed smell is often found on railway embankments.

Passage of time: years later on the same road I am the parent and the driver and the initiator of travel activities for the children. Andrew counts all the harrier hawks north of the Waitaki; chalks up a running total in the dashboard dust.

Travelling this road alone, as I often do, brings on its own set of diversions and rituals: mental calculations of average travelling speed, kilometres to run, ETAs, favourite stopping places for a cup of thermos coffee among the yellow flowers of broom on the braided bed of a salmon river, or beside a backwater full of musk and water speedwells. So many of the riverbed and roadside flowers seem to be yellow – wild brassicas, lupins, dandelions, gorse – in harmony with the yellow road lines and the AA signs.

The beauty of gorse in the landscape is tempered by the knowledge that one is observing the flourish and often the spread of a problem weed. As a people we are collectively too slack to prevent even the most obvious of weed take-overs, because we do not deal with the *invaders*. Weeds like gorse are here to stay. But being mostly a weed does not negate its beauties.

Purple linaria, *Linaria purpurea*, along the railway tracks at Addington, Christchurch.

Consider TIME again. Leap forward a thousand years. What sort of roads, vehicles, energy sources, and roadside flowers will there be? Can you see the remains of a nation-wide network of graded, gravelled embankments: the railways? The last train would have long passed. The last railway station turned craft shop would have gone. The first fibre optic cables would have had many replacements. But might you still see, I wonder, the pattern of today's railway plants, fennel and purple linaria?

Weeds on the seedy side

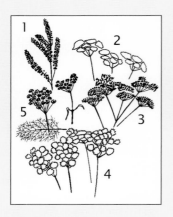

1. Curled dock, *Rumex crispus*.
2. Hemlock, *Conium maculatum*.
3. Parsnip, *Pastinaca sativa*.
4. Cow parsnip, *Heracleum sphondylium*.
5. Fennel, *Foeniculum vulgare*.

These are tall weeds from roadsides just north of Dunedin though, with the exception of the cow parsnip, they could be collected almost anywhere in the country. The curled dock in this picture is a more red-headed form than usual. All the other plants are in the carrot family, having tiny flowers in umbels – flower heads that are like a repeatedly branched rotary clothesline.

One way to be a successful weed is to produce masses of seed. And one of the strategies for massive seed production is to be a biennial, like three of the plants shown here. Hemlock, parsnip, and cow parsnip use their first year of growth to concentrate a store of food reserves in a taproot. In year two, all this food goes towards producing as many flowers, and ripening as many seeds as possible, before the parent plants die.

We eat the taproot of parsnip, but only in its first year, before the plant has gone to flower. The tall yellow flower heads of wild parsnips can often be seen on grassy roadsides. Cow parsnip, Heracleum sphondylium, *is a plant to be avoided. It is known with certainty that its close relative,* Heracleum mantegazzianum, *the giant hogweed, a biennial that can reach 3.5 m tall, can cause blistering dermatitis when skin contact is followed by exposure to sunlight. Parsnip* foliage can affect some people in the same way.

Hemlock is also poisonous. Fennel is not, and can be eaten as a herb for its strong aniseed flavour. Few of us would set out to eat docks, though they probably wouldn't do you much harm, and indeed the leaves are useful for rubbing on nettle stings. From time to time, dock seeds turn up as an impurity in bread which has a wheat-grain coating, the pyramidal black seeds of the dock having been harvested along with the wheat.

9 *Canterbury Tales*

The wildflowers of Canterbury are those which thrive on stones and dust and hot air. The stones are the by-products of shattered greywacke mountains, strewn by gravity and rivers across wide valleys and broad plains. The dust comes on the nor'-wester, the wind which having dumped its rain on the alps, then blows hot and dry and blustery, fraying flowers and tempers.

Like most of New Zealand, indeed most of the world, the history of Canterbury could be told in terms of a sequence of invasions: physical, biological, and human. There have been invasions by grasses, iwi, runholders, rabbits, sheep-stealers, exotic conifers, weeds and wildflowers. The Canterbury Tales told by the following wildflowers are arranged to illustrate their different stages and intensity of invasion.

Pinks, *Dianthus plumarius*: a line-up of flowers from near Otematata, to show some of the variation in colour, pattern, shape and frilliness of the petals.

Pinks have gone wild from gardens onto a few favourable sites, such as dry banks and gravelly road cuttings, on the Port Hills and up the Waitaki Valley, places where there is not much competition from other plants.

One place where you can find plenty of white campion is near Omarama, on roadside and riverbed; no doubt it will spread further in future. This and other campions got their name *Silene* after the god Silenus, who was always drunk and covered with spittle from the mouth, as campions can be covered with a viscid secretion.

Russell lupin, in many colours, has been deliberately planted, some of it in recent years by a grasslands scientist, David Scott, to add diversity to sheep diets. In earlier years it had been planted by Scott's mother to add colour to the high country landscape. Lupins have now found their own way up and down the braided riverbeds. Pretty they may be, but because they clog the riverbed habitat of rare birds, large areas of lupin now need to be controlled. Californian poppy is another plant that loves a gravel riverbed. The warmth of early summer days is needed to fully open the flowers, usually a brilliant fiery orange, but sometimes cream or yellow.

White campion, *Silene latifolia*, at Omarama.

Russell lupins dancing for the nor'-wester in the Mackenzie country.

Russell lupin, *Lupinus polyphyllus*,
near Lake Tekapo.

The invaders that are presently having a field day in inland Canterbury and Otago are the hawkweeds, *Hieracium*. In places they cover virtually all the ground, and the patches that are not hawkweed are rabbit holes or dusty soil laid bare by wind or frost. There are several hawkweeds, mostly ground-hugging mats with yellow flowers. The most widespread ones are mouse-ear hawkweed (*Hieracium pilosella*, which is more of a hawk than a mouse) and king devil (*H. praealtum*, which is more of a devil than a king and would therefore seem to be growing dangerously close to God's picturesque little church at Lake Tekapo). Whence the name hawkweed? It apparently comes from a former belief that birds of prey used hawkweed juice to strengthen their vision.

Californian poppy, *Eschscholzia californica*, on the gravelly shores of Lake Tekapo.

King devil, *Hieracium praealtum*, and thorny bushes of matagouri, *Discaria toumatou*, beside the Church of the Good Shepherd, Lake Tekapo.

Pelargoniums on the Sumner cliffs

Left: Zonal pelargonium, *Pelargonium ✕hortorum*.

Right: Ivy-leaved geranium *Pelargonium peltatum*.

Who says Christchurch is totally flat? The city also has sloping suburbs, upon the lower flanks of the Port Hills. At Redcliffs and Sumner both houses and horticultural wildflowers perch on or above near-vertical cliffs. There are wild window-boxes here, filled with the life and zest and colour of the pelargoniums that have come via the plant breeder, and the garden urn, from somewhere dry and sunny in South Africa. Zonal pelargoniums have a zone of dark leaf tissue, as a semi-circular pattern, hence an alternative name of horseshoe pelargonium. Long live the zonal pelargonium, captain bold of a thousand beach home gardens, and its ivy-leaved cousin that trails pink flowers high up a coastal bank or hedge.

10

Aoraki and the Mount Cook Lily

Mount Cook lily, *Ranunculus lyallii*, in an avalanche chute in the North Huxley Valley, Canterbury.

Mt Cook – Aoraki – is not always kind to its visitors. Too many mountaineers will have had a friend who has come out by chopper or been incorporated in a glacier. Lots of tourists will return without having made a scenic flight, nor having seen the snowfields, nor unpacked a camera. The alpine flowers cannot choose their weather either, and the chances are that even in summer they will unpack their wares on stormy days and lose most of their petals and pollen grains to the rain and snow.

When I went on a little pilgrimage to Mount Cook early one December, I found Mount Cook lilies in flower all right, among the speargrasses and subalpine scrub along the road beside the Tasman Glacier. But the road was awash, the flowers were thrashing about in a gale force nor'-wester, and the camera needed more than a brolly and a tea towel to keep it dry. The photos from that day were fairly hopeless.

The Mount Cook lily is not really a lily, and is not restricted to Mt Cook. It grows naturally right through the Southern Alps and on to Stewart Island. As the emblem of the Mount Cook Line the flower can be seen decorating the back ends of their planes and buses. Nobody seems to be pedantic for long enough to call it by its alternative name "great mountain buttercup". Big beautiful buttercup it certainly is, and well worth careful timing of a trip (November, December especially) to coincide with the flowering of the alpine meadows at places like Arthur's Pass,

My favourite mountain buttercup, *Ranunculus buchananii*, in the Dart Valley, Otago.

Mount Cook, or the Milford Track. It is a summer-green plant, producing a wholly new set of lush leaves, water-lily shaped, every season. Plants reach a metre high when showing off their masses of 5 cm flowers, with petals broad, white, and delicate.

My first encounter with Mount Cook lilies and with real mountain daisies was a memorable fulfilment of hope. A certain love and awe of mountains must have been absorbed into my soul, from having grown up among packs and parkas and mountaineering parents, although we lived far from the real mountains. I got there in stages. One special milestone was my first trip above bushline to the subalpine zone. Jerry Aspinall took me up to Cattle Face in the East Matukituki.

Every ascent to treeline is something of a surprise, for you climb the first thousand metres of your mountain within the innards of an enclosing forest, getting only rare outward and downward glimpses of the view and of your progress. Then suddenly you emerge out into tussock country or subalpine scrub, a quantum gain in visible altitude and a grand entrance into the alpine gardens of nature.

In the early 1960s the alpine flowers were suffering severely from widespread peak populations of deer. Numbers were such that the best hunters in the Otago mountains could achieve huge tallies, like Frank Erceg's best daily total of 107, or Wattie

Cameron's 92. Then in 1965 the Matukituki Valley witnessed the start of helicopter hunting, when Tim Wallis in a lumbering piston-driven machine would drop off bevies of ground shooters, and ferry down whole mobs of slaughtered deer, all bred and fattened on the alpine plants.

On that day with Jerry we had seen the tail-end of several mobs in the bush, at least 80 together in the tussock basin above us, too far away for a shot, but there turned out to be more accessible animals just a couple of minutes over a spur from our lunch spot. What I also saw that day for the first time, were mountain daisies and Mount Cook lilies, even though they were miserably restricted to the few steep ledges and crevices out of reach of the deer.

These days, with deer numbers greatly reduced, at least for a while, the palatable mountain plants have come out of hiding, and again form extensive flowery meadows. New Zealand alpine flowers are a real treat in themselves and several books have been devoted to them. We shall view just a few of them

Yellow mountain buttercup, *Ranunculus sericophyllus*, on Mt Boanerges, Canterbury.

White caltha, *Psychrophila obtusa*, on the Old Man Range, coming into flower immediately the spring snow bank has melted.

in passing, in a selection biased towards buttercups and daisies.

I felt obliged to include *Ranunculus buchananii*, because of its beauty. It has been designed with pulsatilla-like leaves, softly hairy and dissected. I give it full marks for its many overlapping, narrow, white petals, as fine as tissue paper. On top of all that I applaud the courageous setting chosen by this plant to display its delicateness. It grows in the high-alpine zone of southern South Island mountains, often far above permanent snowline, with its roots and fleshy stem among moist shattered rock on ledges and in crevices. *Ranunculus sericophyllus* is another eye-catching, high-alpine buttercup which must cope with a very short growing season. At high altitude the winter snow may not melt until well into summer, so the new foliage and shining yellow flowers are poised to unfold, as soon as the melt occurs. White caltha displays this phenomenon especially well. It must perceive the thinning of its white snow blanket, for it is ready to leap into flower immediately a snowbank margin recedes.

New Zealand has about 17 alpine buttercups, and at least 50 species of mountain daisies – *Celmisia* – typically white with yellow centres. *C. semicordata* is one of the largest, with stiff tufts of silvery-green leaves, their undersides a dense tomentum of white satin. It is widely distributed through South Island mountains, among alpine scrub and tussock. *C. traversii* is very distinctive with its brown tomentum edging the leaves. It has an oddly disjunct distribution, being found on tussock mountainsides at either end of the South Island, but nowhere in between. One theory suggests that it was pushed both north and south by the glacial activity that once occurred most intensely in the central "waist" of the South Island, and even yet, has failed to regain that territory.

Above: *Celmisia semicordata*, one of the large rosette species of mountain daisy, sticking up above stunted scrub of snow totara. Beyond are the Mueller Glacier terminus, the Hooker Valley, and Mt Cook.

Celmisia traversii, Mt Arthur, Nelson.

South Island edelweiss, *Leucogenes grandiceps*, Eyre Mountains, Otago.

South Island edelweiss has no problem co-existing alongside glaciers. It enjoys a mountain crevice filled with rock dust and can be found throughout the South Island mountains as well as on Stewart Island. South Island edelweiss, not too different in general appearance from the well-known edelweiss of the European Alps, is one of four species of *Leucogenes* now described from New Zealand. It is always cheerful because its flower-like heads, with their furry flannel lobes, last for months and months.

Furriness is one way in which alpine plants can retain warmth and resist water-loss. Another strategy is to become a cushion plant, a compact construction of numerous tiny leaf rosettes. Many genera have evolved this habit, none more so than *Raoulia*, which includes the well-known "vegetable sheep" that appear to graze the high screes of dry eastern mountains.

Cushion plants in the alpine zone, Eyre Mountains. Pale plants of *Raoulia youngii* within a mound of *Phyllachne colensoi* (top) and *Hectorella caespitosa* (bottom).

Mountain meadow, Cobb Valley, with yellow flower heads of Maori onion, *Bulbinella hookeri*.

From a mountain meadow

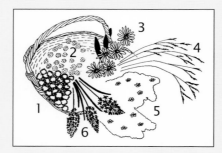

1. *Hebe topiaria*.
2. Cottonwood, *Ozothamnus leptophyllus* (= *Cassinia leptophylla*).
3. Dall's daisy, *Celmisia dallii*.
4. Red tussock, *Chionochloa rubra*.
5. Manuka, *Leptospermum scoparium*.
6. Maori onion, *Bulbinella hookeri*.

A lot of mountain plants are not strictly alpines, but inhabit the montane zone, part way up the hill if you like. These six native plants meet up with each other in the montane zone of North-west Nelson (as well as in a willow basket made by a Takaka craftsman). Three of them you might meet in many districts: red tussock, manuka, and cottonwood in one of its many forms. The cottonwood, although native, is a problem weed in the dry hill pastures of Marlborough.

The other three are restricted to the northern end of the South Island: Dall's daisy (Mr Dall was an early botanical explorer); one of the so-called Maori onions, Bulbinella hookeri (Sir Joseph Hooker was a botanist); and Hebe topiaria (...read on, for topiary explained...).

Diversion into topiary

Topiary is the trimming of bushy plants into weird and wonderful shapes. Hebe topiaria *achieves its ball shape quite naturally, sans secateurs, and is one of many native hebes that are popular with gardeners, partly for this reason. I could not resist including the photo of the truly topiaried yew bush for comparison. As for the whimsy decoration with marigolds: it was not one of my arrangements, believe it or not!*

Hebe topiaria in the Cobb Valley, Nelson.

Yew, *Taxus baccata*, in the Queenstown Gardens.

11 A Bit of Lip

Some flowers have full faces, none more obvious than the garden pansy. Many other flowers have partial portrait features such as eyes, throat, beard, veins, or even adornments resembling acne.

One family of flowering plants is known, and is named, for having a prominent lower lip. The lip or labia (or mint) family has the traditional name of Labiatae, although the strict rules of plant nomenclature favour the formal family name of Lamiaceae, that is the family for which the genus *Lamium* is the type, or anchor-point. Lamia was a celebrated marine monster, a blood-sucking serpent-witch of Greek and Roman mythology.

White dead nettle, *Lamium album*, in Riccarton Bush, Christchurch.

There are lamiums among our wildflowers, some of them very localised like *Lamium album*, white dead nettle, which I have come across only in Riccarton Bush, that odd remnant of native forest which survives within Christchurch and whose kahikatea spires are a good deal older than any of the church spires that point to God from this city of the plains. The name "dead nettle" comes from the resemblance to real nettles, yet the absence of stinging hairs.

Hedge woundwort, *Stachys sylvatica*, at Waitangi.

Useful clues to recognising the mint family are the four-angled stems and leaves in opposite pairs. Frequently the leaves are aromatic, with a whole range of smells. Hedge woundwort has a strange clinging smell – I have seen it described as "like stale lint" and wondered whether that meant a used lint pad at the time of removing an old dressing from a wound. Apparently the name woundwort relates more directly to the usefulness of the hairy leaves applied to a bleeding cut, to help the blood coagulate. Hedge woundwort does grow in the shade of hedges, as well as around forest margins and clearings. It grows erect, sometimes to 1 m tall. Another "lip" plant can be used to stop bleeding and is named accordingly: selfheal (see p. 117).

No wonder the woundwort has lots of smell, for it bristles with tapering transparent hairs, each one with a pink glandular knob at the end, coated with a globule of smell-oil. For a visual treat the woundwort flower is decorated with road maps of white routes upon pink and purple. Each flower is marked a little differently from the next, the sort of variation of blotch and spot that you see in those black-and-white Friesian dairy cows.

Pennyroyal has a strong confectionery smell of peppermint, and has been cultivated for its oil. Butterflies like the flowers. Cows will happily eat the foliage, but dairy farmers can be dismayed when the milk takes a peppermint taint. Pennyroyal grows in the three main islands, most commonly in the North Island. It reaches 30 cm tall, has leaves barely 1 cm long, and is most typical of wet pastures.

Wild basil (Clinopodium vulgare) is really a misnomer, for it lacks virtually any smell, and belongs to a different genus to the real basil which is cultivated as a herb. Wild basil is a straggly low-growing plant of scrubby places, scattered from Auckland to Otago.

To find other members of this family, browse in any herb garden, and also look out for mint, marjoram, and thyme elsewhere in this book.

Pennyroyal, *Mentha pulegium*, and common blue butterflies, *Zizina labradus*, Orongorongo Valley.

Wild basil, *Clinopodium vulgare*, under dry scrub near Picton.

Left: Aluminium plant, *Galeobdolon luteum*.

Right: Bugle, *Ajuga reptans*.

Below: Ground ivy, *Glechoma hederacea*.

A bunch of hoods

None of these hooded flowers is common in the wild. Their most likely habitat is a bush-edge on the outskirts of town. They are all wildflowers of the unwanted kitten variety. They start off as cute and desirable garden treasures, increase to unwanted extent, then end up carted off to the countryside in a sack, to infest some bush reserve or another. I retrieved this bunch from near Dunedin.

Aluminium plant is named for the metallic blotched leaves of the variegated cultivar. The feature that most intrigues me about the yellow flower of this plant is not its tiger-striped lower lip, but its parasol hood, fringed with eyelash hairs. Perhaps they keep the rain from interfering with the reproductive interior of the flower.

12 *A Bed of Roses*

It is said that life is not a bed of roses. What is really meant by this? Our dictionary says "any easy or comfortable place", which in the rose world sounds more like a fragrant bed of pot-pourri petals, than a thorny bed of prunings. Some people grow beds of roses; some people may lie on beds of roses; most simply make use of the cliché.

Roses are like dogs. Whereas there are lots of different breeds closely associated with humankind, not many of them go wild. Most cultivated roses are pampered pets, incapable of reproducing themselves by seed, let alone performing the tricks of budding or grafting that a nurseryman would attend to on their behalf. Few roses become properly wild in New Zealand, in the sense that they form populations that perpetuate from seed. It is the ones with child-bearing hips that reproduce, for the fruit of a rose, usually orange or red, swollen and slightly soft, is called a hep or hip. Hence rose-hip syrup.

Sweet brier, the rose with pink flowers in summer, orange-red hips through autumn and winter, and an apple-like smell, is by far the most common of wild roses, to the extent of being a real nuisance to farmers in drier districts, especially on the eastern side of both main islands.

Dog rose is a similar shrub, less hairy than brier, with the flowers white or sometimes tinged pink. It tends to grow in areas of higher rainfall, and can be seen, for example, on the riverflats of the Waimakariri, at Klondike Corner, near Arthur's Pass. This is the point where the west-to-east motorist (or the sodden motor-cyclist, as I have been, escaping the deluge) often emerges from the pouring rain of a nor'-wester, suddenly to dryness and blue sky in the lee of the main divide. This is the point too where the annual Coast to Coast athletes stop running and start cycling again, though few of them are likely to get more than a sweat-framed view of a dog rose, let alone a nip on the heel.

Sweet brier, *Rosa rubiginosa*, in the Upper Clutha Valley, near Luggate.

A really bright roadside rambler rose at Golden Downs, and a glimpse up the Motueka Valley.

If neither a bed of roses nor a crown of thorns has any appeal, what about a few scratches in return for a bowl full of blackberries, finger-staining good! Available free, through most of the country, for at least half of the year (about November to May), but with varying degrees of palatability.

It doesn't take much imagination to see that blackberries are classified close to roses: look at the blackberry flower and the thorny canes for example. The blackberry, *Rubus fruticosus,* is an aggregate of many entities which in their northern temperate homeland have been classified and named as numerous species. Wild blackberry populations also vary in different parts of New Zealand in their leaf shape, armature, and flower colour, and it seems that this reflects the districts of origin of those pioneer colonists who introduced them. Wasn't it a Crumpy yarn that included the comment that there are only two blackberry bushes on the West Coast – one on either side of the road?

Japanese wineberry is also a *Rubus* and also has edible fruits. It grows along forest margins and in other shady disturbed places, mainly in the North Island.

A house which looks out onto the coast near the famed Moeraki Boulders of North Otago. Does the rose hold up the last of the verandah, or is it the other way round?

Blackberries, *Rubus fruticosus* agg., beside Ngutunui Stream, near Otorohanga.

Japanese wineberry, *Rubus phoenicolasius* in second-growth bush under Mt Taranaki.

Roses from the wild side

Left: The Big Bay rose.
Above: *Rosa wichuraiana* hybrid cultivar 'Alberic Barbier'.
Below: Dog rose, *Rosa canina*.

These roses came indoors to be photographed on a day that suddenly turned wet and stormy. They had also come in from the cold at an earlier stage, in the sense that I had propagated them from wild places, and reintroduced them to garden life.

The term "old rose" is used to describe rose cultivars of yester-year, along with the original rose species from which they were bred, as distinct from the popular and fashionable rose cultivars of recent decades. But their oldness is relative. Thus the "old" rambling rose 'Alberic Barbier' dates from 1900, the year in which it was bred, in France, by M. Barbier. By that time the rambler, which for want of a reliable identification I simply call "the Big Bay Rose", was already some 30 years abandoned in a former garden in remote South Westland. When gold prospectors settled at Big Bay one Robert Cleave opened a store for a few years in the 1860s. I suspect it was Cleave who planted the rose at the former settlement, for a horticultural interest shows up in his later seed and nursery business in Invercargill. Over a century later, Graeme and Anne Mitchell propagated more of the rose to grow beside their whitebaiting and deer-hunting home at Big Bay, and from there I brought cuttings back to Dunedin.

Of the three in the picture, the small-flowered dog rose, is by far the oldest, being one of the 150 or so species of Rosa, this one originally from Europe and south-west Asia. Rosa canina has played a significant role in the horticultural history of roses, as the hardy rootstock onto which other more desirable rose cultivars are budded. Should the rootstock produce its own leafy shoots, and its own flowers and fruits, it is then equipped to jump the garden gate and go seek its fortune in the world at large.

13 Food for Thought

We don't seem to eat a lot of flowers, wild or otherwise, which makes you wonder how many potential flavours we are missing out on. Cauliflower is one we eat, though I suppose what we are really munching is caulibud. One gardening friend says that if you get tired of eating the leaves of silver beet, that good old standby of a vegetable, then let it go to flower and eat the bunches of flowers and buds of the upper stems: much better he says. I can further suggest looking for the beet plants that can be found wild on some Marlborough beaches; that way you don't even need to dig a vegie garden, nor let it run to overmaturity.

What about eating real flowers? Whenever our local food co-op has a bit of a do, there are salads with the flower power of borage and nasturtium (see p. 91). No doubt the same flowers still appear in the alternative salads of Tryphena, Takaka, Westport, and Waitati.

Once I grew spider orchids (see p. 158), which were a timely novelty for a twenty-first party to which all the guests had been instructed to wear a flower. When the night wore on and the compulsory party trick of eat-your-flower was sprung upon us, I found my delicate little orchid a much easier morsel than did the two guys who had grabbed a whole hydrangea head each, at the last minute, on the way up the front path.

Opposite page: A flower you can eat – borage, *Borago officinalis* – a garden plant which appears also in waste places, or decorating a salad. So-called "blue borage honey" is not derived from this plant, but from the much more abundant viper's bugloss (see p. 62), which is also in the borage family.

Kaikoura coast – coast of koura, of good kai, good food – and our own little slice of Monte Carlo raceway, where Marlborough rock daisies, *Pachystegia insignis*, perch on the cliffs above the motorist.

Pachystegia in the process of letting its fluffy paragliding seeds fly off to their own rock crevice.

Kaikoura kai moana and a seaside salad

1. Parsley, *Petroselinum crispum.*
2. Spearmint, *Mentha spicata.*
3. Kareko, karengo, purple laver, *Porphyra* sp.
4. Paua, *Haliotus australis.*
5. Kowhitiwhiti, watercress, *Rorippa microphylla.*
6. Puha or sow thistle, *Sonchus oleraceus.*

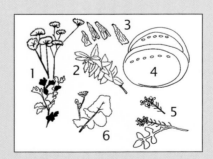

Despite being fresh from the seaside or the sea, not each of these incredible edibles can lay equal claim to a place in a bunch of wildflowers. Yet what diverse delights they offer. Look at the colours revealed inside the paua shell when you have shucked off the leathery black and white part of the animal with your thumb. Yours are the first eyes to see the beautiful curved rainbow ceiling which the paua could not see, and had kept to itself for its many years. What is the purpose of the colours?

Chew on a piece of kareko, the membranous purple-green seaweed of the high-tide rocks and imagine the decorative flowery way its close relative amanori is wrapped around steamed rice in Japan. Think of the flavours if not the flowers of parsley and puha that grow on the Kaikoura coastal rocks; and the mint and the watercress from the nearby ditch beside the road.

These days the Maori name puha applies to several species of Sonchus, most of them naturalised from the northern hemisphere. The original puha, the native Sonchus kirkii, with rosettes of greyish leaves, is also an edible feature upon this coast, growing on rock stacks among the raucous and splattered gull colonies.

Because the Kaikoura mountains rise straight from the sea, both road and railway vie for the confined space between surf and cliff base, and they both dive in and out of short tunnels where the local custom seems to be to try out your car horn and its echoes. Good fun, and you can personalise the acoustic test with a good "yahoo" or an "eehah" out the window.

Travelling this coast by car can sometimes be a mad rush to or from the Cook Strait Ferry, but often enough we have managed an overnight stop or a decent sort of dally somewhere near Kaikoura so as to catch a low tide, don the face mask and snorkel, and satisfy some remnant of hunter-gatherer instinct by collecting a few paua for a feed.

The most attractive sea food alternative of the Kaikoura coast is, of course, the koura itself, the creature subsequently known by the names crayfish, New Zealand rock lobster (euphemism when exported to United States markets), and rark larbster (change in pronunciation once it gets there). Signs along the Kaikoura roadside simply call them "cooked crays", and really good tucker it is too, once you've made the decision to fork out some dollars. As they say, "just do it".

Today the Kaikoura coast markets whales as a visitor attraction, in line with the modern attitude of protecting and even revering the few of these huge creatures that remain. Not so very many years ago we were still revering the whalers. The Tory Channel whaling station produced a type of kai moana, that I remember seeing in open lorries in Picton in 1954, as big cubes of whale meat, the darkest red-black of meats, destined as kuri kai or dog tucker. Was it a component of "Fido" I always wondered. Did the brotherly taunt, "go on, let's see you eat a bit of the dog's food" also mean eating a bit of whale?

14

Sand Between the Toes

For Christopher Robin, sand between the toes was one of life's basic pleasures. Who else has memories of the simplicity of barefoot holidays at the beach? Sand in your socks, all through the hut, sand in your hair, sand in your sleeping bag; what the hell!

Consider William Blake's opening lines to 'Auguries of Innocence':

> To see a World in a Grain of Sand
> And a Heaven in a Wild Flower,
> Hold Infinity in the palm of your hand
> And Eternity in an hour.

How many of us might have had the timeless, absorbing pleasure of lying on a Westland beach, on a dune still being warmed by the very late evening

Flower heads of
pingao.

Pingao, *Desmoschoenus spiralis*, covering the sand-dunes
at Coal River, Fiordland.

sun before it dips into the sea, having created a sandcastle bedecked with sticks and shells, flowers and leaves that form such fantasies as the main trunk line, Raurimu Spiral, Otira tunnel, Mapoutahi Pa, and the last furlong, around which to have obstacle races with those fat caterpillars which live on the shore bindweed roots?

I have had the good fortune to visit remote beaches in Fiordland, where you can see rare examples of original dune vegetation. I think of Transit Beach, where sand made of pink garnets sets off the blue-grey foliage of native sand spurge (*Euphorbia glauca*). I think of Coal River, a jewel of a beach, guarded by a sometimes dicey surf-landing and by a reputation, which I can confirm, of intense swarms of sandflies.

Coal River was named for the black appearance of its sand-dunes, these being composed not of coal but of hornblende, magnetite, and ilmenite crystals. Upon the black dunes is a vastness of orange-golden pingao, the rough-leaved sedge endemic to New Zealand, much prized in the weaving of Maori tukutuku, a taonga now being rediscovered, re-valued, and replanted, up and down the country.

Pingao was one of our main sand binders; the other, especially in the north, was spinifex grass (see p. 60), with silver hairy leaves and tumble-along seed heads. Today the introduced marram grass has been deliberately planted or has invaded far too many of our foredunes, often pushing out the native sand-binders.

Tree lupin, *Lupinus arboreus*, on the dunes of Victory Beach, Otago Peninsula.

Purple groundsel has added new colour to modern beach scenes, though the flowers are sometimes white instead of purple. Already widespread, it nevertheless has a patchy distribution and has a good deal of spreading and infilling to do yet.

Poor old tree lupin, so-called, is not much of a tree really, reaching two metres tall or three at the most, and having wood that breaks and rots very readily. Flowers are pale yellow or sometimes off-white. This Californian plant with the heady summer scent has colonised most of our coastal sand-dunes, as well as gravelly and silty inland riverbeds. It has been a useful plant for adding nitrogen to the soil, and for giving livestock some extra nibbles. Tree lupin didn't seem to mind getting eaten by caterpillars of the native kowhai moth, but in recent years it has been severely knocked, especially on the coast, by a disease-causing fungus.

Ngaio is a mostly coastal tree, often growing with sand between its toes, and recognisable from the leaves being densely dotted with almost transparent glands. The tarry black leaf buds are distinctive too. My childhood introduction to ngaio came about by helping Frank Denz, a toxicologist neighbour, to strip these sticky buds off armloads of ngaio branches. He used the buds for his experiments on the toxicity of ngaione, the poison responsible for periodic deaths of livestock, especially cattle. Nowadays, as a gardener, there is a different substance that I regularly associate with ngaio. It is the fresh smell of cut branch ends, encountered during pruning, a smell which reminds me of lemonade.

The other *Myoporum* in the picture is an Australian one, boobialla, often planted in New Zealand as a bushy shelter plant, sometimes even by mistake for the native species. Occasionally it becomes naturalised along the coast. It has green leaf buds, slightly narrower leaves, and smaller flowers with fewer purple dots than does our native *Myoporum laetum*.

Two coastal trees compared: the New Zealand ngaio, *Myoporum laetum*, (left) and the Australian boobialla, *Myoporum insulare*, (right).

Long Beach collection

Who remembers making sand saucers full of flowers and other objects in their childhood? Who didn't have a backyard sandpit littered with petals and plastic wheels, clods and clothes pegs and cat scats? These days even real beaches have their share of plastics, and more than their share of introduced plants. This is an arrangement of the most conspicuous sand-dune plants from Long Beach near Dunedin.

1. Sow thistle, *Sonchus oleraceus*, from Europe to W. Asia.
2. Tree lupin, *Lupinus arboreus*, from California.
3. Purple groundsel, *Senecio elegans*, from South Africa.
4. Marram grass, *Ammophila arenaria*, from Europe.
5. Poroporo, *Solanum laciniatum* (native, also in Australia).
6. Shells of tuatua, *Paphies subtriangulatum*.

Cook's scurvy grass, *Lepidium oleraceum*, in fertile soil beside penguin burrows on Green Island, off the Otago coast.

15 *Salt of the Earth*

Left: Bachelor's button, *Cotula coronopifolia*, and the reflected stems of oioi or jointed wire rush, *Leptocarpus similis*, in a brackish puddle, Hoopers Inlet, Otago Peninsula.

Below: The salty estuary of Lake Grassmere and the dry ranges of Marlborough.

One high summer in student days I shared the peak of the flowering season with the alpine flowers of the Routeburn track, and the mixed personalities of fellow track workers, Max and Conway, Bob and Bruce. It was the last-named who expressed his yearnings for city food, with deliberate philosophical gems such as, "You know... if we had some fish, we could have fish and chips... if we had the chips... 'cos we've got some salt".

Many summers later I camped beside Lake Grassmere, probably the saltiest part of New Zealand, aside from that class of fish and chip shop which uses a salt can with a shower rose for the heavy-handed shake. Grassmere is a big coastal lagoon in Marlborough, the sunniest part of the country, with nearby Blenheim recording over 2400 hours of sunshine per year. It is an ideal place to evaporate seawater in big shallow ponds, and produce common salt to titivate the taste buds and harden the arteries of a nation.

All plants which grow near estuaries and tidal rivers, on sand-dunes and coastal cliffs, must tolerate salty soils, and high salt concentrations in their tissues. Some must cope with having the salt crystals that have been wind-dried from the ocean surface, blasted into their foliage during dry storms. Because the seeds of many coastal plants can survive a journey in seawater, they have the ability not only to migrate around our own coast, but also to make longer ocean voyages. For this reason many of our native coastal plants are found also in Australia, and some of them we share with Japan, Africa, or South America.

Cook's scurvy grass is different, a native restricted to New Zealand, and now rare. It is not a grass in the modern sense of the word, but a cress, slightly mustard-tasting but quite palatable, and formerly abundant enough for Captain Cook's crew to gather by the boatload as a way to prevent scurvy, and as a green vegetable to relieve their salty diet. Introduced browsing animals have also found it palatable which is one of the reasons it is now mostly restricted to inaccessible coasts and offshore islands.

Beside Lake Grassmere

Provided you have your own supply of fresh water, there is a spot suitable for an overnight camp on the dunes between the shallow salt ponds of Lake Grassmere and the sea. The regular campers here, lined up behind a row of wind-shorn macrocarpas, are a motley line-up of old boat-launching tractors. From here you watch the sun set beyond parched brown hills and hazy ridges of the Kaikoura Ranges. By long evening we explored the dry dunes and the damp dune hollows, and by calm morning made these two collections of the wildflowers.

From the sand-dune:

1. Marram grass, *Ammophila arenaria*, with the rat's tail flower head.
2. Knobby clubrush, *Isolepis nodosa*, with the mace-like, pincushion heads.
3. Harestail, *Lagurus ovatus*, a softly hairy dune grass.
4. Spinifex, *Spinifex sericeus*, the native dune grass with silvery leaves, showing the orange stamens of the male flowers.
5. Native celery, *Apium prostratum*, can be used to add both flavour and saltiness to a salad.
6. Sow thistle, *Sonchus oleraceus*, once again: this plant turns up in lots of places, but it never seems to look much good in a photo.

and from the dune hollows:

7. Beard grass, *Polypogon monspeliensis*, usually found in damp or salty places.
8. Sea rush, *Juncus kraussii* var. *australiensis*, a rigid, dark-flowered rush, of estuary mud flats.
9. Marsh clubrush, *Bolboschoenus caldwellii*, another estuary plant, with 3-angled stems, and a flower display that is mostly the dangling cream stamens.
10. Salsify, *Tragopogon porrifolius*, is sometimes grown for its edible, parsnip-shaped root. The daisy flower heads open in the morning, but close up again in the afternoon.
11. Sand sedge, *Carex pumila*, occurs naturally through much of the Pacific. Its corky seeds, greenish with a yellow-brown suntan, must travel well on the ocean waves.
12. Strawberry clover, *Trifolium fragiferum*, has a particular tolerance of salty places. Flower heads become inflated, fluffy, and strawberry-shaped as the seeds ripen.

16 *Picnics in Marlborough*

Marlborough must indirectly contribute a lot to kiwi picnics, for its plants transform a lot of sunshine into party fare. Grapes are turned to wine. Viper's bugloss nectar becomes honey. Marlborough garlic and olives now contribute to the national cuisine. The most interesting metamorphosis happens with barley, the cereal grass that fills whole fields and sometimes spills wild onto roadsides. Most of us probably never give a thought to barley and how we use it. But consider this energy sequence: sunshine becomes photosynthate in the grass leaf, later to be stored as starch in the ripening grain of the barley seed. When the seeds are germinated their starch is converted to maltose, a sugar intended to nourish the new seedling. By intervening at this point the brewer ferments it instead, to make alcohol for beer and whisky, leading inevitably to one or another form of well-being, frivolity, and aftermath. A very popular extra twirl on the carbon cycle.

As the centre of this grape-growing and wine-producing region, Blenheim has a popular wine (Blenheimer) named after it, though nobody seems to be certain whether to pronounce the product in pseudo-German, or so as to rhyme with enema. There are many possibilities for picnics in Marlborough. From Blenheim you can join a vineyard tour. In Picton you might choose the grass under the Canary Island date palms where the town frontage faces out to Queen Charlotte Sound, or you might head up one of the roads that wind through second-growth bush and where purple-top, yarrow, and bracken and tree-fern fronds frame the views towards scrubby hills and distant arms of inland ocean.

Barley, *Hordeum vulgare*, inside the barbed wire fence, and viper's bugloss, *Echium vulgare*, out on the long acre, near Blenheim.

Beauty and the Beast

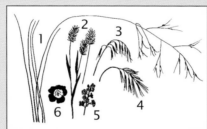

1. Nassella tussock, *Nassella trichotoma*.
2. Rough dogstail, *Cynosurus echinatus*.
3. Barren brome, *Bromus sterilis*.
4. Downy brome, *Bromus tectorum*.
5. Catchfly, *Silene gallica*.
6. Sweet brier, *Rosa rubiginosa*.

Life may not always be a picnic, or a bed of roses. Nor is botanical fieldwork always so. Disbelievers back in the city or the office may well ask "how was your holiday?" after a field trip, which invites an answer that emphasises the long days, sandflies, rain, or frustrations. Nevertheless, there are days when the dictates of the job in hand lead you to unexpected but delightful places that no amount of planning or imagination would have got you to, places where fieldwork food is well earned, and lunch a truly personal picnic.

Accordingly, I find myself sitting alone on the gravels of a Marlborough riverbed, partly shaded by a willow tree, beside tinkling river ripples, with a spicy pottle of last night's rice and vegetable dish, a plastic spoon, and a can of fruit juice. What brings me here is the weedy grass nassella tussock. My colleague Henry Connor, a grass taxonomist, has described Nassella *as the nastiest of weedy grasses. Yet in flower,* Nassella *is one of the loveliest of grasses, its florets purplish and fine, upon silvery threads that waft and shimmer in the lightest of air movements. "Like gossamer", I was told by the man from the Nassella Tussock Board, the body then responsible for seeking and grubbing out this South American grass which has been invading dry parts of the South Island since at least 1905.*

They are a catchy lot, one way or another, this bunch of dryland weeds. The thorny wands of sweet brier usually catch me in the scalp and ears. Catchfly earns its name by trapping small flies and floating fluff on the glandular hairs of the calyx. Nassella seed heads catch a ride on the wind, sometimes in tumbling masses that accumulate against fence wires or even in the power lines. The seeds of brome grasses and dogstail catch their ride by sticking into fur or pelt or clothing.

17

Capital Collections

Marguerite, *Argyranthemum frutescens*, Wellington Harbour.

"Airport cabbage", *Brassica fruticulosa*, at Wellington Airport.

Wellington: terminus of trains and boats and planes, city with an airport for a door mat.

To Wellington: early morning flight, from the south. We have climbed through the blind innards of a wet southerly, leaving below the remains of a dawn that had held uncertain prospects for air travel. Out the window on my left, someone has left a bootprint and the mark of an oily hand on the trailing edge of a grey wing. These become the foreground of my view, across untrampled hills of cloud, too soft to walk on, extending a great distance towards the long white alps. Inside our flying cocoon, inclined to their magazines and papers, are rows of mostly men's heads, ones with grey hair, clean hair, oily hair, or still-slightly-wet hair, heads that ignore the safety instructions, heads that jiggle with the turbulence, or turn towards the appealing smile of the "would you like a lolly sir" attendant. A crinkle of wrappers is audible above the rush and hiss of wind and engines and ventilation.

Approaching Cook Strait, we bounce down through sandwiches of cloud and sky. I catch a glimpse of our Lake Grassmere campsite, and get a measure of weather direction from the streaks of wave spume on the ocean road directly beneath. How many other of the passengers might be looking out for a whale or a UFO? How many of them see Wellington's welcoming sweeps of flowers on its coastal cliffs – yellow bone-seed or white marguerite daisies. The pilots must get a brief impression anyway, and cannot help but notice in early summer, the hill flank of Miramar blotched orange by mats of gazania daisies,

and later, purple with drosanthemum.

Airports differ markedly in offering opportunity for a decent walk between flights. From Wellington you can at least get down to the shore of Cook Strait near the south end of the runway. Otherwise you quickly find yourself caged out from the next-door greenery of golf course and hillside. But some exercise can be had by pacing the high netting fence, with one eye to the possibilities of the larger ragged holes, and with another to the plant which I call airport cabbage, for this *Brassica* seems especially common here. It should not be confused with all the other sorts of airport cabbage, inside the terminal buildings. Instead it has similarities in flower colour with other wild and cultivated brassicas, which include turnip, rape, mustards, and cabbage, the real thing.

Spur valerian can be found in many cities, but I cannot help thinking of it as being especially typical of the waysides of Wellington. Perhaps that is why it crept into both of the group photographs. Its flower colour ranges from pink to magenta, and sometimes to white.

Oriental Bay

No city could be more appropriate than Wellington for inspiring a book called Gardens in the Wind. *Some of these Wellington cliff dwellers are among the plants which author Jacob De Ruiter recommends for difficult coastal conditions. They combine colourful display with a toughness to wind and coastal storms. They put on a public showing on the steep banks above the harbour, easily seen if you share your lunch break with the joggers and the gulls, round at Oriental Bay.*

There is one native plant in this collection, the coastal shrub taupata, renowned for seaside hedges, and having orange fruits to feed the birds. All the others have foreign accents.

From the Mediterranean we have spur valerian and Tangier pea, a scrambling annual that is less hairy than the familiar sweet pea of gardens. Mile-a-minute is another pea-family scrambler, seen here with white flowers though they range to pink and purplish, as we shall see later on Rangitoto. It is South African, and so is bone-seed, the yellow-flowered daisy shrub. The other two (the shrubby marguerite daisy and the succulent pinwheel aeonium) come from the Canary Islands, in the North Atlantic off the Sahara coast of Africa, a floristically special place that has given us and the rest of the world many horticultural and wildflower novelties.

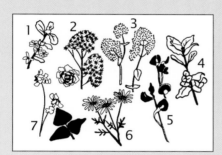

1. Bone-seed, *Chrysanthemoides monilifera*.
2. Pinwheel aeonium, *Aeonium haworthii*.
3. Spur valerian, *Centranthus ruber*.
4. Taupata, *Coprosma repens*.
5. Tangier pea, *Lathyrus tingitanus*.
6. Marguerite, *Argyranthemum frutescens*.
7. Mile-a-minute, *Dipogon lignosus*.

Bolton Street Cemetery

Bolton Street Cemetery is not all it once was. This inner city cemetery, just a short walk from the high-rise heart of Wellington, was bull-dozed through for a motorway. So much for the "final resting place" of those who were at the bottom end of the burial ground. You might call this a mature cemetery. It has jungly parts with thickets of trees and shrubs. Old-fashioned roses have been planted in lots of the plots. Flowering bulbs have had many years to expand into sizeable clumps. The photo was taken in October during the brief flowering season of the bluebells, and the harlequin flowers in their many colours.

On looking up the Flora to identify *Sparaxis tricolor*, I was interested to see that the first record of it growing wild in New Zealand was from this same Bolton Street Cemetery. My late colleague Ruth Mason had collected it there in October of the year I was born. Ruth made a lot of interesting plant collections from cemeteries, places where the horticultural fashions of yester-year start becoming the wildflowers of tomorrow.

Perhaps because the picked flowers last so well in water, arum lily has an association with funerals, so much so that one gardener I know refuses to grow it for this reason. Periwinkle grows in many cemeteries, as a dense knee-high mat with mauve flowers. Mexican daisy especially enjoys a mature cemetery, for over time, cracks and crevices in the masonry become increasingly common, providing more and more habitat to its liking.

1. Periwinkle, *Vinca major*.
2. Arum lily, *Zantedeschia aethiopica*.
3. Bluebell, scilla, *Hyacinthoides non-scripta*.
4. Mexican daisy, *Erigeron karvinskianus*.
5. Spur valerian, *Centranthus ruber*.
6. Harlequin flower, *Sparaxis tricolor*.

18 *Social Climbers and Hangers-on*

Old man's beard,
Clematis vitalba,
on Bluff Hill, Napier.

By the law of the jungle there are three main options for plants to achieve a place in the sun. You can be a tree, a percher, or a vine. While the trees do it with a trunk, having to invest much of their energy into wood, the vines are hitch-hikers, snaking and looping and grasping their way up into the treetops, there to sprawl their own foliage and flowers upon that of the trees, as selfish solar panels.

Some weedy vines can exclude so much light that they smother and kill the very trees which support them, such as old man's beard will do to even the tallest of kahikatea trees. An awfully vigorous plant, the old man's beard is a *Clematis* from Europe. In the 50 years since it was first recorded growing wild in New Zealand, it has spread along valley floors especially, upon fertile alluvial soils, where it will blanket the rounded forms of willow trees and climb to the tops of the last remnant river-bank totaras. Its other name is traveller's joy; maybe the seeds feel joyous as they disperse by air, each floating on a silver feathery pappus.

Bomarea caldasii, Otago Peninsula.

The social climbers profiled below are treated roughly in the order you would meet them, going from the temperate south to the subtropical north.

Invaders of native bush in the south, Chilean flame creeper and bomarea both come from South America. They share the ability to sprout new shoots from underground storage stems, so neither is bothered by being slashed or frosted back to ground level. Both creepers are enticingly attractive in flower: easily taken into cultivation; regretted later.

Opposite page: Chilean flame creeper, *Tropaeolum speciosum*, at Bucklands Crossing, North Otago.

Banana passionfruit, *Passiflora mollissima*, near Dunedin.

Imagine if we had hummingbirds here, the proper pollinating partners for the outward-facing, long-throated flowers of the Chilean flame creeper. Imagine what birds might have been attracted to its brilliant cobalt-blue fruits in its native land. Chilean flame creeper belongs in the same genus (*Tropaeolum*) as the garden nasturtium (see p. 91). *Bomarea* is a climbing relative of *Alstroemeria* (see p. 123) and you can see the similarities in the leaf shape and the clumps of tubular flowers.

Banana passionfruit also comes from tropical South America, and although it is now cultivated in many lands, it has become a serious weed only in Hawaii and New Zealand. In the photo you see the fine tendrils which arise from the leaf axils. Initially the tendrils are outstretched as they wave about, seeking to loop around the

Native bindweed, *Calystegia tuguriorum*, Otago Peninsula.

Below: Great bindweed, or convolvulus, *Calystegia silvatica*, Nelson.

first item that they touch. Once contact is made, another coiling takes place, the tendril effectively becoming shorter by spiralling tight like a phone cord. Flowers and fruits can often be seen at the same time, the flowers pink and pendulous, and the fruits positively dangling as if to tempt a hand to pull them off. The fruits are straighter than most bananas, but yellow and elongated enough for the common name analogy.

In both the native bindweed and the introduced great bindweed or convolvulus, it is the main aerial stems which do the spiralling and climbing. As many weeding gardeners will know, there are extensive underground stems too: white, rubbery, with the ability to regenerate from the smallest of any broken fragments left in the ground. The typical trumpet-shaped flowers of the bindweed family are seen also in blue morning glory. Every day a fresh batch of flowers demonstrate both their common name and the brevity of life. In early morning the flowers open a glorious brilliant blue. During the afternoon an underlying red colour shows through more and more strongly, until by

Blue morning glory, *Ipomoea indica*, at Opua, Bay of Islands.

evening the flowers are purple. By this time they have also become withered and twisted, spent squibs, limp and damp. Every brand of film I have tried records not only the blue which so pleases the naked eye, but also the underlying redness in the flower. So don't ever be satisfied merely to look at photos of this plant; go seek your own early morning glories, on a misty Bay of Islands summer, in those stolen hours before the crowds get up.

Japanese honeysuckle and jasmine share several features. Both come from Asia. They are both climbing shrubs with lovely fragrance, widely cultivated, but they occur in the wild mainly in the northern half of New Zealand. The flower of Japanese honeysuckle is initially white then changes colour to creamy yellow. Jasmine does a colour switch too, from pink in the bud to white in flower.

Moth plant, yet another liane from South America, escapes from cultivation mainly in the North Island. Sticky secretions in the flowers will trap moths and other insects, hence the alternative name of cruel plant. Breaking a leaf or stem reveals a milky latex, typical of this mainly tropical family (Asclepiadaceae), and seen also in the related swan plant (*Gomphocarpus fruticosus*) which people grow as the food plant for monarch butterfly caterpillars.

The great tropical family, Bignoniaceae, contains many climbers with large showy flowers, including Cape honeysuckle from South Africa. This is used as a hedge plant, especially in the northern half of the North Island, and though it seldom sets seed in New Zealand, it can make dense thickets when left untended to layer and ramble, or when it sprouts from discarded prunings.

Japanese honeysuckle, *Lonicera japonica*, on Tiritiri Matangi Island.

Jasmine, *Jasminum polyanthum*, near Leigh.

Moth plant, *Araujia sericifera*, at Kaitaia.

Cape honeysuckle, *Tecomaria capensis*, Northland.

Bush lawyer has curved prickles for clinging onto tree limbs. The prickles of this vicious, blood-letting vine also grab hapless bush travellers, usually by the soft skin of cheek or ear or inner arm. At least real lawyers do not actually draw blood when they get their claws into your back pocket.

It is seldom easy to take a social climber down a peg or two; perhaps more fun to see them falter and topple when their supports give out. Likewise climbing wildflowers: they do not lend themselves to being picked and placed artificially upright in a vase, for they wilt fast, performers no more in high places.

Bush lawyer, *Rubus cissoides*, near Dunedin.

Two native clematis

Left: *Clematis foetida.*
Right: Puawhaananga, the lady of October, *Clematis paniculata.*

For much of the year clematis goes unnoticed in the native bush, the foliage scrambling high and hidden upon trees and shrubs. Spring fragrance draws attention to the yellow-green flowers of Clematis foetida, *and fallen white sepals on the forest floor make you look upwards for the wonderful waxy flower displays of* C. paniculata, *the most showy of the eight or so natives. Most* Clematis *species are climbers or scramblers, which hang on by looping their leaflet stalks round any stem or twig which they touch.*

19 Heath and Heather

A Scots lass, who came to Otago to do a PhD., was pointed out to me at a seminar as "Heather who's working on hazel. Or maybe she's Hazel who's working on heather." Indeed she was the latter, and she studied under a Scots Professor of Botany, Peter Bannister. P.B. we call him, being both his initials and his job description. Come to think of it, New Zealand botany seems to have more than its share of Peters!

Funny things, names, and the ways in which they associate people with their callings. Another PhD. student, Jake Keogh, who is about as spindly and Irish as you could get, did his thesis on wild Irishman, the thorny native shrub known also as matagouri. A pair of ecological colleagues, Colin Meurk and Martin Foggo once co-authored a paper on the vegetation of misty Campbell Island.

I have never actually met anyone called Erica, but have met the plant genus. *Erica lusitanica*, the Spanish heath, is our most widespread weedy heath, from Northland to Southland, able to grow on thin soils that can see-saw between being waterlogged for parts of the year and baked dry in a drought. It is a shrub with white flowers, tinged pink in the bud, turning brown while the seeds ripen. There are over 600 ericas, mainly South African and Mediterranean, many of them grown in gardens.

The term "ericoid" is used to describe many similar plants having small, narrow and dense leaves, while the word "heath" is also applied to more than just the members of the erica family. Thus manuka, although in the rata family, has ericoid foliage, and often grows in heathland with

Heather, *Calluna vulgaris*, on the Volcanic Plateau.

Spanish heath, *Erica lusitanica*, near the Waiuta gold mines, Westland.

Manuka, *Leptospermum scoparium*, at Matapouri, Northland.

other wiry, small-leaved, and fine-rooted shrubs.

Most of us know manuka in the wild as having white flowers, that appear *en masse* in summer as if the scrub had been dusted with icing sugar, a contrast with the stems so often blackened by sooty mould. Bright colours are common in some manuka populations, especially in the far north, where manuka often dresses itself in shades of pink or red. Manuka is pungent in more than one sense, having sharp-tipped leaves, and an acrid taste. Hence its use as a substitute for tea, and its other name, tea-tree. South of Dunedin a little place that was once a railway station, became known by this name, yet with the pseudo-Maori spelling of Titri. As I said, funny things, names.

Manuka, pink-flowered, at Waitiki Landing, Northland.

Under the volcano

Before ever visiting the central North Island I was aware of its wild and unpredictable reputations. How, from time to time, its mountains veritably blow their tops. How a lahar spewed down a volcano side could wipe out a railway bridge. How winter motorists could be trapped on its "Desert Road".

What a fitting place to let loose a few more agents of wildness. The Volcanic Plateau is where budding tank drivers get the feel of making tracks in tussock grasslands and upland bogs. It is where contorta pine has blown wild, where herds of horses have been given free rein to free-range so they might have the odd starring role in TV ads, and where 80 years ago, one John Cullen, so-called park caretaker, persisted against all reasoned opposition, in sowing the seeds of heather and the seeds of trouble into Tongariro National Park. His idea was to make a place for game birds, grouse especially, from the old country. Today: no grouse but any amount of heather, pushing through and over the tussocklands, romping pinkish-purple like the excesses of a careless

1. Heather, *Calluna vulgaris.*
2. Bracken, *Pteridium esculentum.*
3. Red tussock, *Chionochloa rubra.*
4. Bell heather, *Erica cinerea.*
5. Manuka, *Leptospermum scoparium.*
6. Harebell, *Wahlenbergia albomarginata.*
7. Grassland daisy, *Celmisia gracilenta.*

spray painter, millions of tiny flowers, billions of tiny seeds. Motorists can unwittingly assist their spread by picking a flowering sprig that has seeding capsules attached, then discarding the whole item out the window, further down the road.

When we went hunting for heather round the skirts of Mt Ruapehu, we had the bonus of finding bell heather as well, another straggly sub-shrub from Europe. The white-flowered things in this bunch are natives, the shrubby manuka, and two of our commonest mountain meadow plants, the grassland daisy and the harebell. The frond of bracken is a young one, pinnules still rolled, koru-iti, its hairdo still in curlers. The fluffy heads of a red tussock got into the picture too. They look better, of course, on the living plant, among the fine wands of leaves that waft in the slightest breeze or surge and wave when the wind gets brisk.

20 *Moving up the Coast*

Pig's ear, *Cotyledon orbiculata*, on the sand-dunes, Mount Maunganui.

On this leg of our jaunt we hive off to North Island beach resorts, ports, and other sorts of seaside attractions, each with its own display of flowering immigrants.

Although less of a large mountain than its name would suggest, Mount Maunganui stands out as the landmark entrance to Tauranga Harbour. "The Mount", in everyday language, has a big reputation as a place for a beach holiday, or to retire in the sun. One plant that also enjoys the Bay of Plenty lifestyle is an orange-flowered succulent from South Africa, called pig's ear. The genus has been called *Cotyledon*, presumably because the opposite, rounded leaves resemble the first pair of seed leaves (the cotyledons) of many seedlings. Often a garden outcast, pig's ear can be found on coastal rocks and sands from Auckland to Otago. An attractive plant, even when not in flower, its green leaves are overlaid by a dense white bloom, and set off by a red perimeter line.

Century plant has succulent leaves of a different sort, up to 2 m long and with spiny margins. Although a century is overstating the case, the huge rosette does wait a decade or more before flowering. Suddenly and rapidly, all its resources go into a flower stalk that may reach 10 m tall, a lofty candelabra bearing yellow-green flowers. The rosette dies after flowering but is replaced by young offshoots. Among the places where you cannot miss this plant are the cliffs of Bluff Hill overlooking the port of Napier, or on the sand-dunes of Hot Water Beach, that remarkable place on the Coromandel where a hot spring allows you to have a warm wallow on the sand. Century plant is an *Agave* (try "ag-ar-vee" for pronunciation), and it is easy to believe, from its growth habit, that it comes from Mexico. Other *Agave* species are used to make the alcoholic drink tequila, and the fibre sisal.

Our next succulent also has interesting connections, being quite

Opposite page: Century plant, *Agave americana*, beside Aotea Harbour.

similar to *Aloe vera*, the cure-all plant with the well-known name. We are looking at *Aloe saponaria*, a spotty-leaved, spiny rosette scattered along the coast from Northland to Canterbury, and yet another South African by birth.

A choice place to visit a wild rock garden is Rangitoto Island, youngest of Auckland's volcanic cones, its profile the essence of so many views from the city. There is rock aplenty as rough and raw scoria. Soil appears to be nil, which seems merely to please the pohutukawa trees. Holiday cottage gardens near the boat landing look happy with neither soil nor watering system, and the successful plants scramble into the bush edge and down to the sea shore. There are drifts of aloes, crassulas, sedums, and the scrambling vines of mile-a-minute. Now there's a plant with a speedy name. Might it make the ideal complementary companion to the century plant?

Aloe saponaria, Rangitoto Island.

Mile-a-minute, *Dipogon lignosus*, Rangitoto Island.

21

North of the Bombay Hills

Auckland has many faces, and new ones just keep on coming to this "City of Sails", "City of Sales", this "Queen City". Botanist Alan Esler has worked out the rate at which new plants are being added to the wild flora of the city: one every 88 days on average.

My own association with wildflowers of the Queen City singles out memories of a summer spent in Parnell. From the back of the house we faced a distant view to the pine tree and the monument of One Tree Hill, Maungakiekie, set against puffy regiments of bright-faced, dark-based cumulus clouds. Our foreground view was a back lawn that fell away, past a pile of pruning discards, into a gully of tropical looking trees. Down in the gully was a carpet of garden nasturtium, its saucer leaves and orange flowers scrambling rampant over the loose scrunch of discarded paint tins, corrugated iron, and bits of car bodies. Lots of Auckland's history, and its wildflowers, must lie in its rough gullies. The nasturtium is just one of at least 600 flowering plants that have become naturalised in urban Auckland.

Auckland was a Lord, surely, not a Queen, or was he both? Just how queenly is this city? Certainly if you head up the hill behind Queen Street, you come upon Queen Victoria in her Albert Park, cast in bronze. She stands in the scattered company of Sir George Grey, and a marble goddess whom I first encountered in fancy dress, the morning after a party: she had been given one of those toy noses on an elastic band, an orange lion's snout to be precise. These grand ladies look out over carpets of white lawn daisies (*Bellis perennis*) which run

Ivy-leaved toadflax, *Cymbalaria muralis*.

beneath the huge spreading crowns of Moreton Bay figs. There is a marble soldier too, dressed for South Africa, with marble cannonballs underfoot. Once when I was visiting, one of his hands was missing – amputated, shot-off, or souvenired, who knows – but never mind, I thought, for there is a supply of hands nearby, on the monkey hand tree, down a little pathway with a scoria wall, on which you find one particular assemblage of Auckland plants, the oxalis, the toad flax and the knotweed.

Ivy-leaved toadflax and pink-head knotweed both love a rock wall, a cliff, a quarry face, or coastal bank, somehow gaining rootholds in the finest of cracks and crevices. Bermuda buttercup is one of at least a dozen *Oxalis* species naturalised in New Zealand. They are soft plants with clover-like leaflets which fold down at night. Gardeners know them as the foes of ongoing battles. Children know them from the sharp taste of oxalic acid when the stem or leaf is nibbled. The vegetable which New Zealanders call yam – the South American oca – is also an *Oxalis*.

Cape weed is a common daisy in Auckland and indeed through much of the North Island, in lawns and grassy places. It is a smaller and paler relative of the bright-flowered gazanias and arctotis that are grown in gardens. Cape weed has a capital C, because it comes from The Cape: the Cape of Good Hope, southern point of Africa.

Right:
Pink-head knotweed, *Polygonum capitatum*, on a rock wall in Albert Park, Auckland.

Bermuda buttercup, *Oxalis pes-caprae*, in Albert Park.

Gravel groundsel, *Senecio skirrhodon*, at Hobson Bay, Auckland.

Cape weed, *Arctotheca calendula*, on Mt Eden, Auckland.

Picnic bench by the Manukau

Around Auckland you are never far from an expanse of harbour with the green fruits of mangrove floating on the tide, sharp oysters underfoot, and the cosmopolitan call of the kingfisher from somewhere high on an overhanging tree. These roadside flowers, all typical of Auckland, were photographed at Laingholm, beside the Manukau Harbour, one of those places with easy access to an estuary bay head, where people come to walk the dog or catch a fish or spill barbecue fare down their fronts, people in a hurry wearing fancy jogging gear, or those with floral shirts and bright lava-lavas who seem comfortable to spend time standing and gazing, over the tide and the mudflats, towards harbour and horizon.

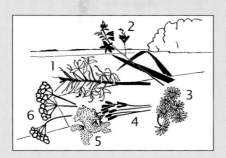

1. Kahili ginger, *Hedychium gardnerianum.*
2. Montbretia, *Crocosmia* ×*crocosmiiflora.*
3. Oxeye daisy, *Leucanthemum vulgare.*
4. Purple-top, *Verbena bonariensis.*
5. Wild carrot, *Daucus carota.*
6. Fennel, *Foeniculum vulgare.*

22

Potatoes Drive In

Above:
Small-flowered
nightshade,
*Solanum
americanum*,
at Totaranui.

Woolly
nightshade,
*Solanum
mauritianum*,
at Kerikeri.

One of the odd signs which repeats itself through the kiwi countryside is the one which reads "potatoes drive in". Is this a definition of potatoes? Or the horticultural equivalent of "pigs can fly"? Are overseas visitors confused by this sign and if so, is there some international symbol that would help?

The potato family produces some lovely fruits. We all know capsicum, tomato, and tamarillo as edibles. But the Solanaceae in general have many toxins, so the fruits of all wild and weedy members should be treated as poisonous.

Small-flowered nightshade is presumed to be native to New Zealand, though it grows also in many other southern and Pacific lands. It is a weedy sub-shrub of open, disturbed sites. The photo shows its flowers like those of the potato in miniature, and the perfect black spheres of the ripe fruits.

Woolly nightshade is a weedy shrub or small tree, having a furry coating on most of its parts, a coarse tobacco smell, usually mauve to purple flowers, and bunches of fruits like yellow marbles. It comes from Brazil and Uruguay, and has become an abundant weed of paddocks and bush edges, especially so from Auckland northwards. White-edged nightshade is a very bold shrub, with veined and spiny leaves, white flowers that you would hardly notice, followed by fruits like hard yellow tomatoes. Apple of Sodom is another prickly scrub weed, in the northern half of the North Island. The origin of the plant is northern Africa, of the common name I'm not sure, though the fruit arrangement is suggestive.

You may find boxthorn living up to its name as a prickly small-leaved hedge, nowhere more characteristic than surrounding the dairy paddocks of coastal Taranaki. Its seeds can fly, thanks to the attractive red packaging of the fleshy fruit and to the courier services of birds. So you are also likely to tangle with boxthorn shrubs where they have become naturalised near the beach and on dry coastal hillsides.

Apple of Sodom, *Solanum linnaeanum*, Rangitoto Island.

White-edged nightshade, *Solanum marginatum*, Otago Harbour.

Angel's trumpet escapes from cultivation via discarded vegetative material, and adds its fruity evening scent to town fringes and waste places from the Bay of Plenty northwards. Thornapple has a smaller flower that is held horizontally instead of hanging down. It has a patchy distribution in waste places and among cultivated crops. This is the plant I once was conned into buying in an Indonesian flower market, "Hey Mister, you want buy palm seed, orchid seed? I give you good price". The palm seed looked genuine, and some of the other seed germinated okay but grew into this white-flowered thornapple weed.

Cape gooseberry has edible fruits, yellow and sweet, hidden within an inflated and persistent calyx, like a paper lantern. People as well as birds help to disperse the seeds around the outdoors.

Angel's trumpet, *Brugmansia candida*, at Leigh.

Thornapple, *Datura stramonium*, at Mapua, Nelson.

Boxthorn, *Lycium ferocissimum* (ferocious indeed), on the Wellington coast.

Cape gooseberry, *Physalis peruviana*,
on Karikari Peninsula.

Copper butterfly,
Lycaena rauparaha,
on cape gooseberry.

Bullibull and Batatas

Left:
Poroporo, *Solanum laciniatum.*

Right:
Potato, *Solanum tuberosum.*

If you put together the flowers of the introduced potato and the native poroporo it is at once obvious that they are closely related. Both belong to the genus Solanum, *both have gained overseas experience far from their homes, and both have had funny things happen to their names.*

Poroporo in Maori became bullibulli to pakeha tongues. As children we knew bullibull for its fat oval fruits, which could be picked so cleanly from the stalks, as ideal ammunition for a shanghai. As a university student I learned that poroporo produced a chemical of use as a precursor for birth control pills. Our botany professor, Geoff Baylis, had an interest in the taxonomy of the native solanums, and this somehow led to his growing experimental plots of poroporo for one of the drug companies. My pocket-money job was weeding the rows, picking the ripe fruits, then cleaning the seed by squashing and washing it free of orange flesh and fibre. Poroporo became widely cultivated in eastern Europe, and I remember the surprise that Geoff shared during one morning tea. A postcard arrived with a stamp depicting the purple flowers of Solanum laciniatum, *this native plant of New Zealand (and southern Australia), yet on a 10 kopeck stamp, from Russia.*

Potatoes came to New Zealand as early settlers, arriving by boat, and on more than one passport. The first arrival was the sweet potato: the plant called batatas in its South American home, and later known as kumara by the time it had finished travelling as baggage cargo through the tropics and the Pacific islands. Its botanical name is Ipomoea batatas, *and it belongs in the bindweed family, Convolvulaceae. Now when the ordinary spud, Solanum tuberosum set sail, also from an origin in South America, it somehow acquired the batatas name, which became potato.*

Solanum tuberosum, the plant which became known as the murphy from its adoption as a staple in Ireland, arrived in New Zealand in the sailing whaling ships. Here it was expertly market-gardened by the Maori who used at least 30 further names for the good tuber. Perhaps it is leftovers from those mahetau gardens which persist in the sand-dunes over the hill from our home.

In the home garden, potatoes are not grown as ornamentals although the white flowers are often used as a signal for harvesting time. Potato flowers can often be seen also in those waste places where someone has discarded garden rubbish, over roadside banks, and around huts and campsites.

23 Somewhat Nasty

Although I hesitate to label any group of plants as nasty, even some of the prettiest have their detractions. Among this lot, somebody at some time has included words like curse and devil in the plant names.

Lantana is a tangled or scrambling shrub, with coarse leaves and stems. To push through a thicket of lantana is to end up somewhat dusty as well as abraded. Nevertheless it has scented foliage, and attractive flowers which change colour from cream or yellow initially, to bright orange or shades of pink as they get older, giving two or more colours in the same flower head. Lantana has become a very widely distributed tropical weed. It has fleshy blue-black fruits, so that birds attend to its dissemination where gardeners leave off. New Zealand is not tropical enough to have a major problem with lantana; it occurs mainly north of Hokianga, and is scattered as far south as the Bay of Plenty.

Lantana, *Lantana camara*, at Leigh.

Mexican devil, a weedy daisy, also shows its subtropical inclinations, by doing its thing in the warmer end of the North Island. It is a tall herb or sub-shrub, found especially on roadside cuttings, and along streams and tracks through bush areas, adding patches of white flossy flowers to the greenery, as it displaces the native forest floor plants.

The name Paterson's curse is sometimes applied to viper's bugloss, *Echium vulgare*, the blue-flowered thing of dry areas (see p. 62). The plant which most often takes the name Paterson's curse is *Echium plantagineum*, a softer plant with slightly larger flowers, less abundant, and found mostly in warmer districts. The curse label on this plant is scarcely applicable in New Zealand; nor is it a universal judgement in Australia. Richard Eyre Patterson (1844-1918) was a grazier, occupying various properties in New South Wales, one of which has been regarded as the source of spread of this weed detested by all cattlemen on the upper Murray. My uncle Basil from Canberra tells me that in parts of South Australia having low rainfall, the plant is seen as useful sheep tucker at the end of a dry spell when

Mexican devil, *Ageratina adenophora*, near Ngunguru.

Paterson's curse, *Echium plantagineum*, near Waiuku.

Alligator weed, *Alternanthera philoxeroides*, at Kaitaia.

Opposite page: Inkweed, *Phytolacca octandra*, at Paihia, Bay of Islands.

all the grasses have gone. There it is called Salvation Jane, for the flower shape resembles the bonnets worn by Salvation Army lasses.

Alligator weed comes from Brazil. At least we do not have alligators as well. But like the reptile, the weed is amphibious. It floats as a mat on slow waters and is also capable of wandering up the riverbank and across moist paddocks. It is recognisable by its opposite leaves and papery white flowers, and can be expected anywhere north of about Thames and the Waikato mouth. Biological control has been initiated in New Zealand, with the recent release of two organisms – a beetle and a moth – which specifically attack alligator weed.

The nasty features of inkweed are that it is

poisonous, causing contact rashes in those who are sensitive to it, and that the fruit juice will stain, should you be silly enough to sit on a ripe plant in your best pale trousers. The flowers are small and whitish; not shown in the photo. We see instead the intriguing sequence of colours from the unripe green fruits, to the inky ripe ones, to the fleshy pink tepals exposed where the oldest fruits have departed. Inkweed hails from the mountains of tropical America and grows in New Zealand from Northland to about mid-South Island in cutover bush, rough pasture, and waste places.

The main disappointment you might have with wild carrot would be to pull one from the ground, recognise the carrot smell and shape in the pale

Wild carrot, *Daucus carota*, at Kerikeri.

taproot, then to find it lacking in edible quality or size, a miserable *Daucus*. What the wild carrot offers instead is a delicately constructed flower head, a branching system where the construction modules are like the radial ribs of an umbrella, yet repeated in a gradation of sizes, the little umbrella skeletons upon the main ribs of the larger ones. This is an umbel, a uniting feature of the carrot family in general.

Before you leave the wild carrot patch, take a look also at the dramatic performance of the umbels, in several acts. The photo shows many of the stages, starting with an inrolled structure that protects the young buds. Next comes an expansion to a pompom or disc of numerous white flowers (but look carefully for the one or more purple ones, in the very centre).

Finally as the seeds ripen the structure again closes inwards via the claw-like bending of the ribs.

Wild carrot grows from Otago to Northland, most abundantly in the north, especially in dry situations among long grass. Another carroty plant with dissected leaves and white umbels has become an abundant pasture weed in Northland. It is parsley dropwort, *Oenanthe pimpinelloides*. We toured the far north by campervan one wet summer, kept seeing this plant from the road, but took it for a small form of wild carrot. Okay, it was raining, and we couldn't be bothered getting wet to check another damned weed. Ironically, we prophesied the scenario whereby a botanist friend said later "didn't you see parsley dropwort, very common". Well, yes we did, but no we didn't!

24 *Towards the Far North*

Garden nasturtium: here at last is a picture of the salad ingredient that got a mention earlier on, my Parnell gully plant (p. 79), and a relative of Chilean flame creeper (p. 68). Garden nasturtium comes from the northern Andes of South America. In New Zealand it occurs all the way from the Kermadec Islands to Stewart Island, especially near built-up areas in disturbed soil, moist or dry, shaded or in full sun, especially near the coast and avoiding the very frosty districts.

The nasturtium photo is near Ngunguru, a town whose pronunciation I imagined and tried to practice before spending a few days there. I need not have bothered too much – the locals simply call it Nungeroo. What a choice place for the nasturtium, all over a heap of slashed branches, dumped down a roadside bank. See the varied colours on the flowers, and make a mental note to pick a bunch sometime, for a blast of colour on the dining table. My words could never describe the flower beauties: find for yourself the tapering spur; the fringe of frilly combs inside three of the petals; the converging guideline patterns that lead your eye down the throat. What a foliage plant too, with its peltate leaves – the stalk being attached near the middle of the underside – and its flat, almost unwettable surfaces.

Garden nasturtium, *Tropaeolum majus*, and the Whangarei coast.

There are half a dozen evening primroses wild in New Zealand. *Oenothera glazioviana* is the largest of them. It escapes from cultivation, most often onto gravel roadsides and riverbeds. The flowers open by evening, and last only for a day. The picture shows it at mid-morning, in Kerikeri, near the famous stone store which was built in the 1830s. We see one droopy flower which finished yesterday, some outwardly-held fresh flowers that opened last night, and enough fattening buds to last a week or so. For ourselves, last night at Kerikeri was an empty section, overlooking the tidal part of Puketotara Stream, among grass that stood tall and sodden wet against the campervan. This morning the rain stopped for a while in Kerikeri. We washed clothes in the tan floodwaters, upriver from the town, but it is too muggy for much drying.

Wattle trees grow along the river scarps, with other bushy greenery. Up behind the prim and picturesque part of the village, natural-looking eucalypts drift along the hillock. I get a feeling of Tasmania. Things get more international in the grassy meadows that run through the gum trees. The assemblage includes wild carrot from Europe, purple-top from eastern South America, Mexican daisy from Mexico, a lily (*Lilium formosanum*) from Taiwan (= Formosa), and aristea from Africa.

How they grow, these field lilies, to 2 m or more tall, with narrow leaves and tapered white trumpets, outwardly arrayed. It seems odd to see a garden-looking lily seeding itself around with ease in the wild. The first wild collection was along a grassy track at Whakatane in 1972. It is known also from roadsides in Auckland city and Whitianga, and on the

Evening primrose, *Oenothera glazioviana*, at Kerikeri.

Rimutaka Range. Recently I discovered it on sand-dunes near Cape Egmont. In years to come we may see more of this plant. On Lord Howe Island, out in the Tasman, it has become the most widespread of weeds on both coastal and mountain ledges.

Aristea grows as a fan of pale green leaves, and has deep blue flowers, each of which opens for just a few sunlight hours. It is locally distributed through Northland and Auckland City, along roadsides and in grassy places.

The name purple-top pretty well sums up an erect plant with square stems and coarse hairy leaves, so often seen in waste places and beside roads in the northern half of the North Island. Purple-top becomes steadily more sparse as far south as Otago.

The 90 km from Kerikeri to Karikari Peninsula take us to sandy beaches where you will see railway creeper, one of those tropical elements in the New Zealand flora, found naturally in Northland, but shared with many Pacific and tropical places. Don't be surprised to see the same plant in Fiji or Queensland.

Lily, *Lilium formosanum*, Kerikeri.

Aristea or blue stars, *Aristea ecklonii*, from Kerikeri.

Spur valerian, *Centranthus ruber*, and admirers, on the rock face overlooking the park and gardens in Whangarei.

Purple-top, *Verbena bonariensis*, with wild carrot, at Whangarei.

Railway creeper, *Ipomoea cairica*, Karikari Peninsula.

25

Retired to the Country

Even after years of faithful service, the fate of some garden plants is to find themselves facing redundancy or retirement. One of their options is to re-train as wildflowers, relocate to quiet warm corners of the country, and then basically do their own thing. Wild gingers and the watsonia have made a real success of the roadside free market.

Both the canna and the ginger families have an oddity in their flowers. The stamens have become petal-like, taking on the showy function of the flower. Large-flowered hybrid forms of canna are commonly cultivated, and can become naturalised. Up north you see clumps of bright yellow, orange, or red, where they have been planted near the farm gate.

Indian shot, *Canna indica* in its wild form, is much more capable of spreading by seed. It does not come from India, the name referring instead to an origin in the West Indies, as well as Central and South America. The seeds are remarkably like shot – perfect uniform spheres 6 mm across, metallic in their bounce, shiny yet finely pitted, and totally black. It is hard to resist collecting a pocketful for later use in pea-shooter or blunderbuss. Whoever fired a blast of Indian shot across our main islands achieved a pattern of successful hits, peppered between Northland and Greymouth. The flower of Indian shot is a flamboyant combination of pinkish-red and yellow.

Indian shot, *Canna indica*, at Kawhia.

Watsonia, *Watsonia bulbillifera*, Houhora.

Canna (a red *Canna* cultivar) and tree privet, *Ligustrum lucidum*, Kaitaia.

Canna (*Canna indica* hybrid) at Te Kao, planted on a farm roadside.

Asphodel, *Asphodelus fistulosus*, near Napier.

Watsonia has a similar distribution, preferring warmer northern districts, and becoming mainly a West Coast plant when it extends into the South Island. You don't have to look underground to see where *Watsonia bulbillifera* got its name. It has bulbil-sized corms, in fragile clusters up the flower stems. These grow readily into new plants, and they spread within soil attached to road-making equipment, or by floating along drains. Watsonia flowers are mostly salmon-pink.

Like the watsonia, parrot gladiolus is out of Africa. Both plants belong to the iris family, and both reach about chest-height in flower, but the gladdy is nowhere near as common, being a slower spreader. I have seen it south of Auckland and in Taranaki. The flowers are red-hooded, over a yellow throat. Gladioli have sword-shaped leaves, and the name is out of Latin, wherein gladius was a sword, perhaps such as a gladiator might have used.

Asphodel is a smaller plant with tufts of fleshy tubular leaves, found from Northland to Otago, mainly on gravelly wasteland not far from the coast. You might need to hunt for this one. The flowers are white or pale pink, 2 cm across, and have conspicuous dark mid-veins on the petals.

Parrot gladiolus, *Gladiolus Xhortulanus*, Waiuku.

Wild gingers

Ginger, with its stubby, hot, and stringy rhizomes, must be one of the more unusual items of flora to have spread itself through the world's cuisine, confectionary, beverages and vocabulary.

For me, an aftertaste of ginger springs from several recesses of the memory. Was there really a "Ginger Mick" of Hokitika for whom so many radio requests were played during that summer I spent in the coal mine on the West Coast? And was the mirth of my mates warranted when the name conjured up thoughts of more than just a red-headed catholic?

Green ginger wine and ginger ale are remembered from a summer trip to the Mutton Bird Islands, away down south. Mixed with whisky, these were our pre-dinner drink ration from the Wildlife Service; the brown-and-dark concoction being termed a "saddleback" in likeness to the rare bi-coloured bird we were working with.

Then there was the summer of the ginger-bread man. That was in the days when full employment allowed students to get a taste of factory life on Cadbury's night-shift. One of the students made a giant gingerbread man from the net-like sheets of biscuit-mix offcuts. Placed on the conveyor belt, the sculpture was sent for baking into the long low tunnel oven, with the intention partly of bucking the boredom, and partly to surprise the packing ladies at the far end. What puzzled them instead was a cessation of baked bikkies to be stuffed into their crinkly packets. By the time this was noticed, some 15 minutes worth of production had piled up behind the well-risen, jammed, and now-burning gingerbread body.

The student got the sack.

"Run, run, as fast as you can, you can't catch me, I'm a gingerbread man." Maybe this storybook line should be transferred to the mischievous wild gingers that have become such pests in New Zealand. They run along roadsides and into bushy gulleys, spreading underground, making chest-high thickets of fleshy stems, each with two opposing rows of lush leaves.

Real ginger, originally from South-East Asia and grown mostly in the tropics, belongs to Zingiber in the family Zingerberaceae. The ginger we eat is the stubby, stringy, swollen rhizome. Our two wild gingers have similar rhizomes, and are in the same family, but are classified instead in the genus Hedychium. The more common of the two, H. gardnerianum, Kahili ginger, can be distinguished by having lemon-yellow flowers, each with a conspicuous red stamen. Through summer and autumn it gives a fruity scent to the evening air. Over winter it puts on a display of scarlet seeds, set against orange linings of the opened capsules. Kahili ginger comes to us from the Himalayas. It is now well-established from Northland to mid-Westland.

Yellow ginger, H. flavescens, has creamish flowers on a shorter inflorescence. It comes from Madagascar and India, and though it does not set seed here, discarded garden plants have formed big patches by vegetative spread alone, especially from Northland to Coromandel.

"Task Force Ginger" is a recent movement to try to eradicate wild gingers from our native bush.

Above: Kahili ginger, *Hedychium gardnerianum*.
Below: Yellow ginger, *Hedychium flavescens*, both at Opua, Bay of Islands.

26 *Aroids*

Among plants, as among people, there are some pretty funny families. The aroids might sound like extra-terrestrial neighbours, but the description does not exaggerate the shapes and behaviour and the evocative names of the arum family, Araceae.

Within the arum family world-wide there are names like skunk cabbage, dead horse arum, Jack-in-the-pulpit, cobra lily, green dragon, *Dracunculus*, and *Amorphophallus*. The actual flowers in most aroids are tiny structures crammed onto a central fleshy peg called a spadix. This is displayed within the partial twist of a flamboyant bract – or modified leaf – called the spathe.

Many aroids have evolved a strategy to attract flies as their pollination agents, not by looking pretty, but by the opposite approach of smelling putrid (the spadix heats up to help volatilize the odours), and by mimicking the bruised or brownish colours, the shrivelled or hairy surfaces, of something in decay. Among the wild and wayside aroids in New Zealand only the stink lily, *Dracunculus vulgaris*, has these features well developed. It will occasionally escape from gardens.

I have not seen it in the wild myself, but a non-flowering plant brought in recently by a Noxious Plants Officer for identification, enabled me to photograph the almost snake-skin patterns of the stem and leaf bases.

As a garden plant, arum lily (or calla lily) can become too hungry for space, which is why both this and Italian arum get dumped down a bank or into a paddock. Left to their own devices they persist as colonies in swampy ground or damp pasture. Arum lily stands up to 1.5 m tall and is very obvious by its white spathes at flowering. Italian arum is a shorter plant, the leaves distinctively dark with pale veins. Flowering could easily go unnoticed. Show time comes with red berries in late summer.

For a long time I failed to find elephant's ear in flower, because I was looking too early in the season. Late summer to autumn is the time. Even then, the yellow-green flowering stalks are insignificant compared to the bold leaves. Strong white main-veins form a raised network on the leaf underside, acting for the leaf like ribs do for a ship's hull or for one's chest. Between them is a fine pattern of secondary veins, in restful curves. Elephant's ear grows as far south as Nelson, as clumps in grassy places and under trees, and has

Stink lily, *Dracunculus vulgaris*, showing the intricate patterning of the leaf bases and stem.

Arum lily, *Zantedeschia aethiopica*, in an old farm garden, Karamea.

the capacity to produce a thick trunk-like stem.

Taro is stubborn to flower and further reluctant to fruit. Perhaps this is because over its long history of cultivation, its reproductive needs have been fully met by gardeners, using vegetative means of propagation. Taro is said to be the oldest cultivated crop in the world, having been grown for 10,000 years in tropical and subtropical Asia. Several varieties of taro came to New Zealand with the earliest immigrants on the first waka. Today some 400 million people eat taro, and it is either a staple food or an important standby for many of them. Taro has a leaf similar to that of elephant's ear, but with a less pointed apex, and the characteristic difference of being peltate – with the stalk attached well inside the margin.

Elephant's ear, *Alocasia brisbanensis*, Kotare, North Taranaki.

Italian arum, or lords-and-ladies, *Arum italicum*, at flowering stage, Dunedin.

Italian arum at fruiting time, tossed over the bank at Kawhia Harbour.

Taro, *Colocasia esculenta*, at the Otara market, Auckland: just the tuber with the leaves removed, and without flowers which you hardly ever see anyway.

27 Legumes Good and Bad

Strictly speaking a legume is a pod, usually elongated, with a seam along the margins, and containing seeds in rows as seen in the familiar broom pod or pea pod. The term legume is also used for all members of the pea family, most of which also share the typical pea flower characters. One pair of petals together form a pointed keel, two more form a pair of wings, and the fifth a flag-like standard, usually erect. Most legume plants have compound leaves with three to many leaflets, and on their roots bumpy nodules, containing *Rhizobium* bacteria, which transform nitrogen gas in the soil into chemical forms that are then available as nutrients for the plants. This is why legumes such as clovers, medicks, and melilots are so useful in increasing soil fertility in pastures. The same feature also gives legumes a competitive advantage in poor soils, so that many – like gorse and broom – have become aggressive weeds in farmland, in native vegetation, along roadsides, and in vast tracts of tractorless country.

Some of our legume wildflowers are garden plants. Although the popular sweet pea does not often become properly wild, some of its relatives, like everlasting pea, will turn up on urban sunny banks. Goat's rue is a useful if somewhat floppy plant which usually stays put in the garden. One notable exception is along the sandy banks of the Manawatu

River which it is transforming into an untamed version of the herbaceous border. Goat's rue is known to be poisonous to livestock.

Lotus is deliberately planted in pastures, as well as in wild places, being hydro-seeded for the stabilisation of freshly excavated road cuttings. It prefers damp ground and has spread into swamps, marshes, and the damp gravels of riverbed and roadside. Leaves having five leaflets help to tell lotus apart from the clovers, which usually have three leaflets.

Not all pea family plants have obvious pods. This is especially true of the peanut plant (or ground-nut; it is not found wild in New Zealand), which thrusts its pods below soil level as the peanuts ripen. In clovers, the pods would not normally be noticed, being small. Woolly clover is one of several species which make themselves especially attractive after the flowers have finished, by the whole head becoming swollen and papery as each individual calyx enlarges around the seed pods.

Everlasting pea, *Lathyrus latifolius*, in Taumarunui.

Broom, *Cytisus scoparius*, near Cass, inland Canterbury.

Broom pods showing off their withered flowers, baby seeds and their hairy edges with the back-light of evening.

A line-up of legume shrubs

As both a food-exporting nation and a tourist destination, New Zealand blithely promotes itself as being "Clean and Green". Does the popularity of this proud boast in the national psyche reflect the effectiveness of the once-common billboard plea, "Keep New Zealand Green"? That slogan was aimed at preventing forest fires, but might its resurrection not be timely, to counter the "yellowing" of New Zealand, as gorse and broom do their merry thing and expand across the landscape?

An old saying says, "Kissing is out of season when the gorse is out of flower". "Never bloomless" said Coleridge, the poet. And although it is true that you can always find gorse in flower at any time of year, it does have two massed flowerings, in spring and again in autumn. These masses of flowers produce heaps of seed, capable of lying dormant in the soil, for several decades as an unwanted "seed bank".

While gorse hedges do have a managed place in the lowlands, and while gorse scrub can in some instances be a useful nurse crop for native bush regeneration, there are nevertheless far too many landowners who regard small patches of gorse as "not a problem", and fail to identify the plants as an invasion, already under way.

The other shrubs in this identification parade are generally less weedy than are gorse and broom. Spanish broom – often cultivated and sometimes a weed of dry hillsides – is an almost leafless shrub to 3 m tall, with stiff, shiny green stems. Tree lucerne becomes a

wild plant on dry hillsides, as well as on riverbeds. It grows to a small tree, very useful as "quick fill" in a large garden, and the foliage is excellent tucker for native pigeons. I have seen it advertised for sale as kereru kai – pigeon food.

Montpellier broom (Teline monspessulana) *is a leafy shrub to 2 m tall, widely distributed in waste places, and especially in sandy scrub along river banks. Teline stenopetala is distinguished by having longer racemes of flowers and is established as a garden escape, mainly on dry coastal banks near cities. This line-up was assembled near Dunedin.*

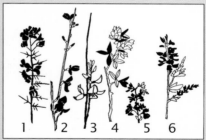

1. Gorse, *Ulex europaeus.*
2. Broom, *Cytisus scoparius.*
3. Spanish broom, *Spartium junceum.*
4. Tree lucerne or tagasaste, *Chamaecytisus palmensis.*
5. Montpellier broom, *Teline monspessulana.*
6. *Teline stenopetala.*

Goat's rue, *Galega officinalis*, on the sandy banks of the Manawatu River at Palmerston North.

Lotus, *Lotus pedunculatus*, beside Hokianga Harbour

Woolly clover, *Trifolium tomentosum*, Omeo Creek, Central Otago.

Clovers to roll over in

1. Red clover, *Trifolium pratense*.
2. Haresfoot trefoil, *Trifolium arvense*.
3. Black medick, *Medicago lupulina*.
4. Alsike clover, *Trifolium hybridum*.
5. White clover, *Trifolium repens*.

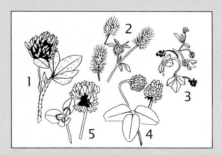

"Roll me over in the clover", says an old song. Clovers themselves must get rolled up, every summer, in hay bales and in those white and greenish plastic intestines of silage that have become part of the rural scenery.

Twenty four Trifolium *species are naturalised in New Zealand. The photo shows four of the more common ones. White clover has prostrate stems that spread across the ground surface, rooting as they go. It can be a nuisance to gardeners, despite being so valuable as a cornerstone of our pasture system. Red clover is a taller and bolder plant, more hairy on its stems and foliage. Alsike*

clover is somewhat intermediate between white and red clovers in its habit and flower colour. All three are widespread and important pasture plants and many cultivars have been bred from them.

Haresfoot trefoil is abundant in dry districts, making its impression more by its furry softness than by the subtle colours of its flower heads. It is easy to see where the hare's foot name came from. Like the true clovers, medicks have leaves with three leaflets, but medicks differ in having markedly coiled pods. It is the pods which are black in black medick; its flowers are small and yellow.

28 *The Red Rata*

Primary school memories include certain images of flowers and other living things. In the early years we had a nature table in one corner, where objects of wonderment could be displayed, but my main memory of that was the day my prized trap-door spider was jealously thrown away by a refugee eastern European boy whose anger I didn't then understand. We later became friends.

Behind the school was a forest of sycamore trees, which provided winged fruits like half-propellers as playthings. Above the trees was a dry bank where rustling skinks could be caught in the long grass and among the heady smell of gorse in flower. The school grounds themselves offered a group of red ponticum rhododendrons with ample numbers of bell-shaped flowers to be threaded onto a string, as a lei.

That activity was best avoided by the boys, for reasons of self-protection, just as Kerry White and I agreed as 8-year-olds not to enter by the same gate after walking to school together, lest we be labelled, girl and boyfriend, da-de-da, da-de-da, by the junior clobbering machine.

Our headmaster, Mr Christensen, a short and portly man in three-piece pinstripe, had some interest in plants and gardening. One of our perks was to be chosen to escape classroom confines by transporting sacks of warmly composting grass clippings from the school to his home garden. Our added reward was food and drinks from his wife.

Every Arbor Day, we assembled outside under the flag, and "Christiepop" would read a speech, the same one every year, which we parroted back, in slow-droned phrases. It included the lines "the red rata (ther... red... rartar), and the golden kowhai". In this way he taught us the importance of planting trees, and imbued us with nationalistic pride for two of the few native examples with showy flowers. Never since have I failed to notice the abundance of red rata and golden kowhai as symbols of kiwi-land, on tea towels, tin lids, tissue packets and postcards.

Of course there is more than one rata and more than one red too. Pohutukawa flowers are described as crimson by many authors, though they can occasionally range all the way to yellow. As the Christmas tree of northern coasts, pohutukawa has a longer festive season than do most holiday-makers, although even outside of Christmas the pohutukawa tree shares its gifts of shade, of low curving trunks to sit on, a handy branch on which to hang your

Pohutukawa, *Metrosideros excelsa*, at Matai Bay, Karikari Peninsula.

Mat rata, *Metrosideros perforata*, flowering low to the ground on the volcanic lava on Rangitoto Island.

Northern rata, *Metrosideros robusta*, in the hillside bush of Mt Burnett, overlooking Collingwood and Golden Bay.

Below: Southern rata or umbellata rata, *Metrosideros umbellata*, on a rain and waterfall day, in the Cleddau Valley near Milford Sound.

towel, and dry twigs to boil the billy or thermette.

Northern rata has darker, brick-red flowers; those of southern rata are scarlet, more of an orange-red. Each of these trees – pohutukawa, northern rata and southern rata – can grow into an ancient giant. But neither their size nor their mana nor their dense red wood – ironwood – can protect any of them from the chomping death knell of possums. A giant castle of a tree needs an extensive workforce for its construction and maintenance: in other words, healthy foliage. Lose this gradually to browsers year after year, and you eventually join the statistics. We are often told what area of tropical forests is lost every day, but has anyone yet come up with a figure for the daily deaths of rata trees?

The mat, or climbing ratas start life as clinging small-leaved mats, which can inch (or centimetre) their way up a tree trunk, attached by little peg-feet to the bark, then spend several centuries with their foliage up in the canopy while the main stem turns into a hanging jungle cable.

Scarlet rata vine is my choice of rata flowers, because I associate it with warm pockets of lush bush near the sea, and with favourite coastal corners in South Westland. Its orange-red flowers seem to glow as they cheer the green bush and feed the honey-eating birds especially in autumn and winter.

Scarlet rata vine, *Metrosideros fulgens*, at Big Bay, South Westland.

Left: Kamahi, *Weinmannia racemosa*.
Right: Southern rata, *Metrosideros umbellata*.

Rata – kamahi forest

In parts of New Zealand where beech trees are absent for various reasons, we often find instead a rata-kamahi forest. Whereas white flowers or pink buds of kamahi can be picked near ground level from bushy young trees, it is not always easy to pick rata flowers, nor always safe as one can suddenly come to realise when a vertigo message comes on, some tens of metres up one of the trunks or out on one of the limbs of an old giant umbellata rata. So my photo settles for rata flowers that had fallen onto the mossy forest floor, which is our usual way of seeing them close-up anyway.

It is ironic that kamahi is so commonly used by florists, yet most of them would have never bought or sold a kamahi flower. Instead it is kamahi foliage we see in the arrangements, for it lasts so well in water.

29

Sunny Nelson

Marble hand among catsear, *Hypochoeris radicata*, on the way over the hill to Takaka.

So-called Sunny Nelson City and Sunny Nelson Region (Sunshine State they call it) boast a good climate for gardening, artistic creativity, and alternative lifestyles. North-west Nelson is a most special place for native plants, having a larger flora than any other part of New Zealand. It has many typical South Island plants, and a big slice of northern ones as well, because the southern limit of distribution for many warmth-loving species is not Cook Strait, as one might expect, Cook Strait having arisen relatively recently on the geological time-scale.

Nelson traditionally produced the nation's hops and tobacco, those specialist crops that once contributed so much to the kiwi culture of beer and fags. Most tobacco farms have now become smoke-free, their high-roofed drying sheds defunct or turned to some other purpose, and the fields converted to other whatevers, maybe mixtures of crops and wildflowers, such as the asparagus and evening primrose combination we came across in the Motueka Valley.

Nelson's fertile plains and valley floors are derived from a wonderful diversity of rock types, including coarse-grained granites, red-weathered serpentinite, sandstones, limestones, and other sedimentary rocks. There are limestone and marble mountains where men have carved quarries, and from which nature has sculpted cliffs, caves, huge sink-holes, and underground streams that emerge as springs of clear water. On the way over Takaka Hill, a sculpted hand emerges from among the roadside daisies, holding a massive marble. A marble marble, mother of all bomb-squashers.

On the coast are giant marbles of a different sort, polished, rolled, and piled by coastal storms, as boulder banks and boulder beaches. Hardly the sort of place you would expect plants to take root, yet a few do manage to reach a smidgen of sand, rotted seaweed, or driftwood fragments, well down among the boulder crevices, plants like the pink-flowered shore bindweed, hugging the sun-warmed boulders at Cable Bay.

Evening primrose, *Oenothera glazioviana*, beside an asparagus field, Motueka Valley.

Shore bindweed, *Calystegia soldanella*, on the boulder beach at Cable Bay.

Buddleia or butterfly bush, *Buddleja davidii*, beside the former cement loading wharf at Tarakohe, near Takaka.

Cobblers from Cable Bay

Cable Bay is where the first undersea telegraph cable linking Australia with New Zealand came ashore in 1876. Lots of people must have communicated with each other in cabled messages beneath this bay. The bay-head beach and storm ridge of rounded rocks and cobble-stones is dotted with these flowers, an unusual assemblage, and one which would most likely recur on a gravel riverbed, shingle roadside, or stony railway embankment, preferably coastal.

From their flowers alone, sand primrose and horned poppy might be confused. Not so from their foliage. The former has strap-like leaves compared with the deeply divided and glaucous leaves of Glaucium, *the horned poppy; horned by virtue of the curved and greatly elongated capsules.*

Wall rocket belongs to the cress family, the crucifers, each flower having four petals in crucifix or cross shape. Again we meet haresfoot trefoil, the furry clover that was in an earlier haybale, with some of its mates (p. 105).

1. Sand primrose, *Oenothera stricta.*
2. Haresfoot trefoil, *Trifolium arvense.*
3. Horned poppy, *Glaucium flavum.*
4. Shore bindweed, *Calystegia soldanella.*
5. Wall rocket, *Diplotaxis muralis.*

Tarakohe limestone lovers

Limestone owes its origins to the undersea accumulation of sea shells and smaller limy marine creatures. Soils derived from limestone are high in calcium and strongly alkaline, providing chemical encouragement for some plants to be restricted to, or especially abundant on limestone. Furthermore, the intricate ways in which limestone weathers and dissolves produces many distinctive micro-habitats.

Under the influences of waves, rain, and gravity, the coastal limestone cliffs at Tarakohe have been shaped to knobbly protrusions, stacks of dinner plates, toppled hunks the size of buildings, overhangs with stalactites, and shady grottos.

Dry ledges are dusted chalky-white. Rock faces and concavities have taken on a black skin of algae and crustose lichens.

Gardeners and farmers know that a dressing of lime can sweeten the soil and benefit plant growth. The plants in this photo, most of them having escaped from gardens, are not species that absolutely demand a limy soil, yet they obviously thrive upon pure limestone, and what sunnier part of Nelson to do so than on a north-facing amphitheatre of whitish cliffs?

The Cotoneaster is a shrub, with small white flowers followed by orange-red berries through autumn and winter. Pale flax, with the pale blue flowers is a

perennial herb with fine stems, found otherwise in grassy or gravelly places. Of lesser stature, but also found in dry grassy or scrubby ground is yellow wort, Blackstonia, a thin erect plant with bright yellow flowers, and a member of the gentian family. Its discovery here at Tarakohe turned out to be the first record of the species from the South Island, which illustrates the ongoing way in which naturalised plants are extending their geographical range.

Garden snapdragons come in many colours. Most wild populations have rose or purplish flowers like these ones. If you squeeze the flower of snapdragon from the side, the mouth will open and close, like that of a dragon. The Mexican daisies in this shot show a similar rich colour as they open but the rays turn pure white when fully expanded.

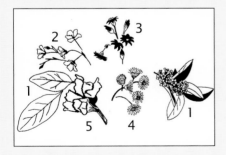

1. Cotoneaster, *Cotoneaster glaucophyllus.*
2. Pale flax, *Linum bienne.*
3. Yellow wort, *Blackstonia perfoliata.*
4. Mexican daisy, *Erigeron karvinskianus.*
5. Snapdragon, *Antirrhinum majus.*

30

Gumboot Country

Gumboot country is my term for wetlands of all sorts – swamps, flushes, mires, marshes, bogs, brooks, and more besides. Over 500 flowering plant species grow in New Zealand wetlands and they can all be seen in the wetland plant book by Johnson and Brooke. I mention this, not only as a brief commercial break, but also to relate two wetland events that arose as the making of that book approached its final stages.

Pat, who did the drawings, was wanting to change her surname away from that of her former husband while retaining the initials PB with which she signed her paintings. One morning we discussed possible surnames that might have a watery connotation. One suggestion was Brook. Well, immediately after lunch, Pat beamed into the office, saying she had done the deed, she had been to the Registry Office, and she was henceforth Pat Brooke.

Having got the authors' names sorted out for the spine, cover and title page, we also needed to arrange an authors' photograph for the back cover. Between Lincoln and Halswell, a stream running beneath a picturesque stone and brick-arched bridge offered a photo opportunity, where I might paddle in the water and Pat might be on the stream bank with her sketch block, attentive to my proffered plant specimen.

Being away from home and having not thought to bring any props or costume for a photo session, I enquired from a colleague whether a pair of tall gummies or thigh waders might be available at the Lincoln campus. "Yes", I was told, "there are some waders in the ecology store. An old pair. They've got lines painted up the sides."

As it happened, these waders were already known to me by reputation, as having belonged to Ruth Mason when she studied lake shore plants and aquatic weeds. One of my sources of information, for example, was a touring American botanist, who had been taken out into the field by Ruth, hunting for *Lilaeopsis*, and he had been especially struck, he told me later, by two things: Ruth's cobwebby Morris Minor (totally un-American in scale and vintage); and by her waders, graduated with these painted lines from which she could record water depth at sample sites.

For the photograph I duly wore the historic waders. Despite their age they were in good nick. No leaks. The major problem was size – or lack of it: about two sizes too small. My toes got in, so did my legs, but my heels remained stiletto-perched: quite a challenge when teetering in a flowing stream among beds of watercress and floating sweetgrass.

Among floating plants my favourite dish is "Pot cheese". Might this be a pidgin term for some savoury recipe? No, it is my usual field book abbreviation for *Potamogeton cheesemanii*, one of the native pondweeds, and named for Thomas Cheeseman, foremost New Zealand botanist for half a century from the 1870s. The oval, floating leaves of this pondweed are usually bronze and are wonderfully unwettable. Prod them under and up they float again. Hidden below water level are the submerged leaves, very different in shape and texture. Membranous and ribbon-like, they are held upon stems that ascend like kite strings from pond floor or lake bed at one or two metres depth. In the photo you may spot a flowering spike, but the flowers themselves are insignificant.

Many of the floating or emergent plants of ponds or river edges are introduced species and some of them have become problem weeds. If you were to paddle into the lower Waikato River you might find yourself tangling with the starry white flowers of wild water lilies, and you might, with imagination, spy Mister Jeremy Fisher or some other croaking amphibian sitting upon one of the floating leaf pads. Or at Huntly, as in the photo, you might well manage to squish across yellow-flowered mats of primrose willow, but would likely be halted by the masses of parrot's feather, a weedy milfoil that came from South America and has spread to many waterways, globally, often as a result of people chucking out aquarium plants.

Pondweed, *Potamogeton cheesemanii*, upper Clutha Valley, Otago.

Primrose willow, *Ludwigia peploides* subsp. *montevidensis*, (foreground) and parrot's feather, *Myriophyllum aquaticum* (beyond) in the Waikato River at Huntly.

I have chosen a native gentian to illustrate a very different type of wetland: *Gentiana amabilis* growing among sedges and a soft carpet of sphagnum mosses on the rim of an alpine bog pool in the southern Garvie Mountains of inland Otago. This is a remarkable "string bog", a peaty landform more typical of sub-arctic and boreal regions, having numerous bog pools arrayed like terraced paddy fields. Most native gentians are white-flowered, in contrast to the well-known blue gentians of European mountains.

A strong contribution to colour in some New Zealand wetlands is made by *Mimulus*. The only native species is *Mimulus repens*, the epithet *repens* describing its creeping habit. Flower size greatly exceeds that of the leaves, and a massed flowering creates purple carpets around coastal lagoons, or in silty, brackish parts of salt marshes. Flowers of the two introduced species of *Mimulus* are yellow. Monkey musk, or monkey flower takes its name from a perceived resemblance of the flower shape to some monkey posture. This tall herbaceous plant grows

Gentiana amabilis in a bog, Garvie Mountains, Otago.

Mimulus repens beside a North Otago coastal lagoon.

best alongside actively flowing streams or in gravelly backwater channels of braided rivers. Musk is a smaller and more sticky-hairy plant of swampy seepages or roadside ditches. The name is something of a misnomer for us because New Zealand populations of this North American plant seem to lack any musky scent.

Monkey musk, *Mimulus guttatus*, beside the Ashburton River, Canterbury.

Musk, *Mimulus moschatus*, in a hillside seepage at Moke Lake, Queenstown.

On a swamp edge

This lot I got near Mot – Motueka, or "mod-oo-acre" as it is called on Nelson Radio. They were fringing a freshwater swamp at the top of an estuary. Walking around in swamps is not as difficult as you might think, once you have overcome the initial daunting prospect of getting your lower parts wet, and having established that there is a reliably firm footing at a certain depth. Swamp travel requires the same energy level and pace as climbing, because you have to ascend at every step, out of the substrate and over the vegetation. Much easier, therefore, to sample the flora, gingerly, from the swamp edge.

1. Raupo, *Typha orientalis*: just the flower heads, tucked in behind.
2. Swamp kiokio fern, *Blechnum minus*, which doesn't have flowers.
3. Tarweed, *Parentucellia viscosa*, so-named for the viscous (sticky) leaves.
4. Willowherb, *Epilobium ciliatum*, a swamp and garden weed.
5. *Carex maorica*, a sedge which grows at the edge of swamp pools.
6. Selfheal, *Prunella vulgaris*: the name *vulgaris* means common, just as the word vulgar describes something commonplace.

Umbrella sedges

The flower heads of two weedy species, and the one native species of Cyperus, *from an Auckland roadside ditch. One of the better-known members of this genus is the tall-growing* Cyperus papyrus, *sometimes grown as an ornamental in New Zealand. This was the plant used by the early Egyptians to make a parchment. Indeed the word paper derives from their papyrus. It was among papyrus sedges that the infant Moses was left afloat and hidden in his basket.*

Left: Purple umbrella sedge, *Cyperus congestus*, from South Africa.

Centre: Umbrella sedge, *Cyperus eragrostis*, from North and South America.

Right: Toetoe upoko-tangata, *Cyperus ustulatus*, native to New Zealand.

31 *A Scatty Bunch*

On looking up scatology in the dictionary I found "interest in the obscene" as expected, but was a little taken aback to realise from the definition "study of excrement, especially to assess diet", that I had myself been involved in the practice of scatology. My role, fortunately not too close to the sticky end of things, was to help identify half-chewed and digestion-resistant plant fragments. They were deer-gut samples from Takahe Valley, Fiordland, which arrived on my bench in stinking little bottles of formalin.

Several wildflowers verge upon the scatological. Mention of *Lavatera*, the purple tree mallow often found on sand-dunes, tends to elicit responses in the genre of lavatory humour. Actually the name commemorates two physicians of Zurich who had the surname Lavater.

The name *Silybum* for the variegated thistle seems to attract the

Tree mallow, *Lavatera arborea*, Otago Peninsula.

same sort of zany wonderment that causes children to make taunting phone calls to people with names like Longbottom. I have learned, via a respected botanical colleague who is familiar with many origins of plant names, that *Onopordum* (cotton thistle), comes from Greek *onos*, an ass; and *porde*, fart.

When it comes to bad smell connotations, New Zealand's stinkwood must have been given one of the worst possible names. As if the genus name *Coprosma* is not enough (*kopros* = dung), this species was further named *foetidissima* ("very smelly"). Field botanists abbreviate the plant to "Cop foet", suggestive of what might be inside Mr Plod's boots. The stink of this shrub, liberated when you brush against the foliage and twigs while bush-bashing, is apparently that of carbon disulphide. At least the flowers don't smell, but nor are they very large or showy, as befits many wind-pollinated plants.

The plant smell which really gets up my nose is that of fireman's helmet (*Impatiens glandulifera*), also known as Himalayan balsam and touch-me-not. The part that resembles an old-fashioned fireman's helmet is one of the sepals, initially shaped like a triangular pocket, and from which the rest of the flower parts emerge.

We grew it in the garden for a few years until discouraged by its bad points. The ripe capsules are poised to explode when touched, the cells being turgid with high water pressure. Seeds are catapulted up to five metres according to some accounts. Even the lightest touch will trigger the explosion: lots of fun, but at the expense of picking up an unwashably persistent stink on the fingers.

Variegated thistle, *Silybum marianum*, near Dunedin.

Cotton thistle, *Onopordum acanthium*, in Central Otago.

Fireman's helmet or Himalayan
balsam, *Impatiens glandulifera*,
Motueka Valley.

Years after banishing fireman's helmet from our garden, we again ran into the plant, and its smell, in two very different ways. By its flowers we recognised big drifts on riverbanks up the Motueka Valley. And we recognised the awful smell again in a bottle of dog and cat repellant, one of those oddities which came our way when mother-in-law shifted out of the family house and into an old people's home. The bottle claims methyl nonyl ketone as its active ingredient, plus inert ingredients, so take your pick as to which portion of the potion has the pong.

Pongs and odours: such triggers to memory. From the public library I borrowed a book on perfumed or smelly plants. Quite a good read too, provided you sat out on the verandah and held the book downwind. A bedside book it was not, for this copy had an overly strong smell. My suspicion was that some previous reader had left the book in the pile of dirty nappies. *Kopros* again!

Stinkwood, *Coprosma foetidissima*, Dunedin.

So far as flies are concerned, the flower fungus, *Aseroe rubra,* might as well be a flower: red with radial arms, and oh, how attractive, especially to a fly. For unlike any real flower which has the attractants of nectar and pollen in the centre, the rays of *Aseroe* surround a spore soup of unmentionable appearance, and having a smell to match.

32 *Wild West*

Westland. The West Coast. The Coast. "Go west, young man": this instruction has led me to some interesting plants and places in the wild west, including trips that have had western accoutrements in the cowboy movie sense, such as wide-brimmed hats, guns, and galloping horses. Actually my slowest trip into Westland was leading a pack-horse down the Hollyford. An unfit, uncooperative, and naughty old nag, she banged into trees, cracking my pack frame and bursting a sack of flour, but she gave me dawdling time to admire the track-side mosses, and thinking time to ponder on how terrible it would be if a road was pushed through this country.

A pioneering spirit persists on The Coast, of people occupying only a fraction of the land, and still eager to forge into the frontiers. A feeling of admiration and possessiveness towards land and climate which resist being tamed, and sometimes expressions of assertiveness against outside opinion or supposed authority that wishes to interfere from "over the hill". A lot of gold has yet to be dug up on The Coast. Plenty of podocarp logs await their turn to visit the sawmill, and a lot of bush gets in the way of development or else threatens to engulf you.

Jack Holloway, forest ecologist, once told me a story, about a West Coast woman walking along the road with a can of petrol, throwing cups full into the bush edge, and followed by a little boy whose job it was to throw lighted matches. Her reply, when confronted, was, "If you'd lived in this bloody bush as long as I've lived in this bloody bush, you'd want to bloody burn it too". This was a hand-me-down story, which, if I remember correctly, originated with Jack's father, the Rev. Dr J.E. Holloway, who was a minister and botanist in Westland early this century.

West Coasters are still battling the elements, especially the rain and all it brings, including floods, rampant vegetation, leached soils, iron pans, rust, and rot. One November I was based in the Maruia Valley. We had seven floods and three fine days that month. Some years later, for a comparable period, the media reported just one spell of rain and a single flood: it lasted all month non-stop. Wool started rotting on the sheeps' backs.

"Falling damp" is a term applied to West Coast rain by a geologist friend, a Coaster who grew up in Hokitika near "great heaps of intimidating bush". Trevor Chinn, a master of both under- and over-

Peruvian lily, *Alstroemeria aurea*, in the upper Buller Valley.

Wandering Jew, *Tradescantia fluminensis*, at the Pororari River mouth, near Punakaiki.

statement, has nevertheless made meticulous measurements of rainfall across Westland. He and his colleagues discovered that annual rainfall in the very wettest zone, some kilometres on the Coast side of the main divide, reaches near a world record peak of nearly 12 metres (or 6 fathoms!) a year. "Send 'er down Hughie".

But, saying goodbye to the rain man for a moment, let us remember that Westland has a mild climate and long stable periods of sunny days: wonderful growing conditions for vegetation. I think of Westland being made of many shades of green, but splashed here and there with redness – of rata crowns in flower in the Otira Gorge, of *Isotachis* liverworts draping moist road cuttings, of sundew leaves in a pakihi or studding the white quartz gravels on the Denniston Plateau, the red shirts of the Kokotahi Band against a backdrop of tree ferns, the orange-red of *Weraroa* pouch fungi among leaf mould, and that translucent red-tea colour you see when dapples of sun penetrate the froth-topped, peat-stained waters of limpid bush streams.

Invading wildflowers are adding a new palette of colours, and my selection of flower pictures takes us on a north-to-south trip through Westland. Bright flowers caught our eye in the Buller Gorge, filling a roadside bush clearing. They were yellow, orange, and striped. Peruvian lily is one of the most hungry spreaders of the several species and many cultivars of *Alstroemeria* to be found in gardens. It is the most likely contender for transfer to a wild place, perhaps with the thought that it is too pretty a plant to be done in completely. It spreads by rhizomes to form patches, with erect stems to about 1 m tall.

Wandering Jew is another cultivated plant, very easy to propagate and grow, easy to chuck out, but almost

Cape pondweed, *Aponogeton distachyos* riding the waves among bamboo spike-sedge, *Eleocharis sphacelata*, at Lake Mahinapua.

Lake Mahinapua

This is a scene which can be seen at many Westland lakes. With the addition of an orange moon or sunset it becomes the focal painting or mural theme in many West Coast public halls or public houses. The nearest pub to Lake Mahinapua is one that used to be known as "The Pu" in my forestry days. Today the tourists are more likely to ask for the Lake Mahinapua Hotel, or that outback pub which gets used for TV commercials.

Back to the lake itself: the bamboo spike-sedge is native to New Zealand as well as Australia, and Papua New Guinea where it is used to make "grass" skirts. It has submerged rhizomes, and erect leafless stems about the thickness of a little finger, and tubular with cross-partitions like a bamboo. Tiny flowers are held in a spike at the very tip.

The Cape pondweed may not look very close or very big in the photo. That is because it grows a bit far out, at a depth where you just start to get your undies wet, and your face too, when you lean down to try and dig out a seedling from the silty gravel with your fingertips. Recently I was asked for a likely location for some young plants, for a woman from South Africa who wanted to grow it; apparently they eat it in her homeland. In New Zealand it grows in lowland streams and lakes, more commonly in the North than the South Island. Cape pondweed has floating, paddle-shaped leaves, and fragrant flowers, held above water level in a distinctive, waxy-white, two-pronged spike.

impossible to kill. So it creeps unnoticed under hedges and trees. Worse still, it smothers the ground in native forest reserves. Every fragment of fleshy stem will take root, and the plant can tolerate deep shade. We found it wandering around the base of coastal flax bushes at the Pororari River mouth, a lovely bit of coast backed by limestone country, and with a tropical feel because of the nikau palms and puka, the fat-leaved broadleaf.

Lots of people stop at Punakaiki for the short loop walk to the pancake rocks and the blowholes. Along the road from the carpark, hydrangeas have also stopped by, as a population that is self-sustaining from seedlings, something which seems to happen only in high-rainfall districts. The shrubs are blue-flowered, an indication that the soil is acid. If the soil was alkaline, as one might have expected at Punakaiki considering the limy nature of the underlying dolomite rock, the flowers would have been pink or reddish. Individual hydrangea flowers may appear oddly flat, empty, and useless. This is because many of the flowers are sterile, especially so on the common round-headed types. Hydrangea plants with the more flat-topped, or lacecap flower head have an outer ring of these sterile flowers, and masses of much smaller fertile flowers in the centre.

At Greymouth we meet corn marigold along the top of the gravel beach, having spread out from the cemetery, where the yellow daisies grace some of the plots, beneath many Irish names, and among multiple reminders of mine disasters and river drownings. The only other place I have seen this *Chrysanthemum*, also in a cemetery, was on the wet west coast of the North Island, at Bell Block.

Hydrangea, *Hydrangea macrophylla*, beside the coast road at Punakaiki. Both mop-head and lacecap forms are present in this wild population.

Corn marigold, *Chrysanthemum segetum*, on the gravel beach at Greymouth.

Indian strawberry, *Duchesnea indica*, Taramakau Valley.

What can I say about Indian strawberry? It does come from India, and eastern Asia. It differs from the real strawberry genus (*Fragaria*) in having yellow rather than white flowers. It escapes from gardens, especially into damp grassy sites, and is most common in wet Northland. When I found it in the Taramakau Valley in December, it had both flowers and fruits on display.

Much of Westland now forms part of the "conservation estate" managed by the Department of Conservation (DoC). Some of it is pristine country, some is hand-me-down habitat which nevertheless retains many natural values despite being pre-owned or cut-over, and of course there are more than enough pests and weeds and other threats to keep DoC busy. One of the minor weeds they can probably afford to ignore is shamrock pea, a clover-like plant but with distinctive large flowers in cobalt blue. You might see it infesting the National Park nature walk at Franz Josef.

Shamrock pea, *Parochetus communis*, at Franz Josef.

A lot of plant knowledge, as well as management advice for Westland vegetation, must have come from two botanical brothers who have also prompted many of my visits to planty places on the Coast. It was John Wardle who caused me once to climb Mt Ranunculus up the Ahaura Valley, and Peter Wardle who instigated our trip to Buttercup Flat astride the Alpine Fault, south of Haast. Good bushmen both these Wardles: they can be relied upon to find waterproof campsites and the best sorts of firewood for the fire. Not such good guides to follow across swollen rivers though: neither can swim, and they tend to wade in, fearlessly.

One of the nice things about knowing one's field companions well is to understand how far they can be pushed by a practical joke. While botanising in South Westland a group of us made a visit to the Haast tip, partly to check it out for wild plants, and possibly also with scavenging opportunities in mind. An unexpected find was two teddy bears, of middling size, identical, and in good condition. By nightfall, they had found their way into Peter Wardle's sleeping bag. Everything went according to plan. Peter spent the late evening poring over maps and air photos with next day's fieldwork in mind and he was the last to come to bed, when the bunkroom was at "lights out" stage. Halfway into bed his bare feet touched something furry with plastic claws. He leapt out, made a commotion and some accusations, and when he thought that everything was settled down, climbed back in, only to discover the second teddy bear at the very bottom of his pit.

What other Teddy Bears' picnics and plants has the Coast offered me?... Delicate, etiolated willow-herbs flowering at the base of a deep tomo in limestone country at Oparara. A dry seat among toetoes on the banks of the Haast River while eating a mountain of whitebait fritters with David Bellamy and a TV crew. Wild radishes and pansies flowering among whale-bone decorations beside Beansprout's hut at Gorge River mouth.

But enough of the wild west. We can leave with the knowledge that it has such renewable resources as possums, sphagnum moss, and lovely sunsets, as we now move on – or back – to Otago.

33

Central Otago Revisited

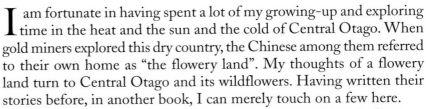

Woolly mullein, *Verbascum thapsus*, on the slopes of Roys Peak above Lake Wanaka.

I am fortunate in having spent a lot of my growing-up and exploring time in the heat and the sun and the cold of Central Otago. When gold miners explored this dry country, the Chinese among them referred to their own home as "the flowery land". My thoughts of a flowery land turn to Central Otago and its wildflowers. Having written their stories before, in another book, I can merely touch on a few here.

Central Otago revisited – yes, and we are camped beside Conroys Dam after a day hunting for a rare grass, *Simplicia laxa*, in shallow caves beneath schist tors on the slopes of the Old Man Range. It is a summer evening, but a cold one. I am glad of my bush shirt. The coffee is hot but tastes too strongly of lake sediment. Such are life's imperfections. But the day is totally reluctant to depart: ten o'clock is still light enough for writing, and for watching the evening rabbits hop and play on hills of yellow stonecrop flowers.

Stonecrop (*Sedum acre*) is a low-growing succulent plant with starry, four-petalled flowers. *Sedum* means sedentary, and this plant sits upon the thinnest of soils, and on stony ledges. You could probably walk overland for 20 kilometres without stepping on much else, all the way from Conroys Dam to the Cairnmuir Range and to Cromwell. History tells us that an armed robbery cache of a thousand pounds may still be hidden on this range. In my youth I wandered these hills, under baking summer sun, searched many rocky nooks and caves and overhangs, flushed quail from nests and owls from shady roosts, found falcon chews, lizard skins, moa bones, merino horns, goat skulls, but no eldorado of banknotes. Surely some rabbit must know somethin'. Which rabbit though? There are so many of the little buggers, which is the reason why the ground has been bared, and why the fleshy and unpalatable carpets of stonecrop have been able to turn the hillsides yellow.

Yellow is the colour also of the flowers on woolly mullein, held on tall spikes above a rosette of flannel-like leaves. Hag's taper is another name for this plant, for it is supposedly used as candles by witches. Maybe that bundle of banknotes has already been unearthed by such a witch with such a candle. Or maybe my eagle-eyed, moth-hunting friend, Brian Patrick will yet come across the money, for last year in a rocky cave-let in Conroys Gully he discovered an intriguing cache of hidden history. It was a neatly folded bundle of women's clothing along with some newspaper fragments dated 1889. Included was a blue, flowery, embroidered jacket with what appears to be a bullet hole in the breast. Tough country this, wherein somebody must once have known somethin'.

Opposite page: Stonecrop, *Sedum acre*, on the hills above Conroys Dam, near Alexandra.

Bannockburn

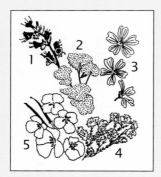

1. Viper's bugloss, *Echium vulgare.*
2. Yarrow, *Achillea millefolium.*
3. Large-flowered mallow,
    Malva sylvestris.
4. Thyme, *Thymus vulgaris.*
5. Californian poppy,
    Eschscholzia californica.

*Crushed thyme takes me instantly
back to Bannockburn;
I knew it would.*

Bannockburn is a dry dusty sort of town, close to Cromwell at the south end of the big inland basin of the Upper Clutha Valley. All these flowers are common along Central Otago roads, and several of them are spread widely across the land, especially the wiry little bushes and the full-on aroma of thyme. For some people it might be possible to know the smell of thyme by sniffing one of the garden varieties or sticking your nose in a dried herb packet, but ah, is it not one of the richnesses of life when a whiff transports you back to the imprinted association with a whole landscape and atmosphere and time of your life? Driving into Central, by whatever route and even in a hurry, there are several winding short-cut roads I know where from the car window I can grab a sprig of thyme, and get a lungful of smell, and a feeling of belonging.

Kawarau Gorge

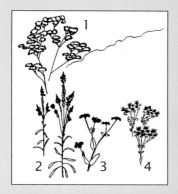

1. Hemlock, *Conium maculatum.*
2. Purple linaria, *Linaria purpurea.*
3. Rose campion, *Lychnis coronaria.*
4. St John's wort, *Hypericum perforatum.*

The Kawarau River ("K'worrer" in local parlance) elbows its way down a valley of shattered schist rock. The water surges a turbulent grey, it boils while yet cold, and has already started to infill with sediment the new Lake Dunstan behind the Clyde Dam (or the dyed clam if you need an alternative name for the biggest and most expensive calcareous shell in the country). Alongside the Kawarau Gorge road, sparkling mica silt, mixed with ancient landslides, makes a loose and fertile soil for natural herbaceous borders. There are two poisonous plants in this group – hemlock and St John's wort – which would not be found in your tidy suburb, but the purple linaria is often grown in gardens, and the rose campion also for its silvery leaves and its shocking pink flowers.

34 *Queenstown*

The resort town of Queenstown attracts visitors to the picturesque scenery and to wild activities such as bungy jumping, skiing, jet boating, or river rafting. More passive and less fiscal forms of R & R include the potential to make forays among flowers. My choices of Queenstown postcard pictures are intended to show both the scenery and the flowers.

My shot of St John's wort is from Twelve Mile Creek, looking down the middle reach of Lake Wakatipu to the Remarkables. The jagged crest and multiple buttressing spurs of the Remarkables Range provide a well-photographed backdrop to Queenstown. The peaks offer shelter to the ski-field in the Rastus Burn, and the high point, Double Cone, must provide a temptation to many actual or armchair mountaineers.

St John's wort, *Hypericum perforatum*, against the Remarkables Range.

Climbers who go solo do so against their own rules, but enough time has passed for me to admit to having done this climb, on my own, with my head literally in the cloud, in the days before the ski-field road took over a thousand metres off the grunt. It was a long way up, from lake level, but it is the long descent I more painfully remember, on account of ingrowing toenails, followed by the youthful hilarity of a Queenstown New Year's Eve, and the oblivion of a few hour's sleep somewhere in the scrub behind the town.

I am not sure which herbal remedies might work for hangovers, but should you be desperate enough upon waking, seedily, among the rough outskirts of Queenstown, you will likely find wild marjoram as the most available culinary herb. I was content not to make a concoction, but have photographed the pink and purplish flowers alongside the road to Moke Lake, with Walter Peak as the scenic setting.

Moke Lake is a delightful place to visit, an intriguing U-shaped body of water where you can watch trout rising and scaup diving to their respective food sources, or where you can lie on a tussocky hillside with your face at the level of the native harebell flowers, white or bluish, and ponder their ungainly name, *Wahlenbergia albomarginata*.

Wild marjoram, *Origanum vulgare*, and a view to Walter Peak.

Native harebell, *Wahlenbergia albomarginata*, above Moke Lake.

Three linarias

Left: *Linaria genistifolia.*
Centre: Purple linaria, *Linaria purpurea.*
Right: Toadflax, *Linaria vulgaris.*

Nice plants these, until you transplant them to the home garden and discover that the two yellow-flowered species in particular are rhizomatous pests. Queenstown is one of the few spots, perhaps the only place in New Zealand, where you can find all three of these linarias growing wild.

Two poppies

Above: Long-headed poppy, *Papaver dubium.*
Below: Field poppy or corn poppy,
        Papaver rhoeas.

Photographing these two poppies together was a race against time. We found them growing close to each other near the marina between Queenstown and Frankton. The day was hot and sunny, and the flowers fully open, but they started to wilt within moments of being picked.

Of the two species, long-headed poppy has the more elongated capsules and an orange hint in the red flowers. Field poppy flowers are usually a pure bright red, sometimes pink or white. Both poppies are annuals which can become abundant in roadside gravel, cultivated soil, or other disturbed ground. The familiar red poppy symbol of Anzac Day is modelled upon the field poppies which sprang up on the shell-shocked World War I battlefields of Europe.

Left: Californian stinkweed, *Navarretia squarrosa*.
Right: Collomia, *Collomia cavanillesii*.

Resinous smells

These two plants sit together as members of the same family –
Polemoniaceae – and in sharing globose flower heads that glisten
with sticky aromatic glands. Californian stinkweed is a stiff spiky
sort of annual herb, usually to about 25 cm tall, found in dry districts
especially in gravelly places such as roadsides. It comes from western
North America. Collomia is South American by origin, from Chile and
Argentina, and is a softer erect herb to 50 cm tall, less widespread
than the stinkweed, but also found in gravels, such as on lake shores.

35 *From Aggies to Irises*

Here is an assortment of flowers from the lily and iris families. Red hot pokers: what fun it was in the days of open fires and coal ranges when you could heat the end of the poker to red heat and burn little pictures and your initials into a piece of wood. Red hot poker plants sometimes squeeze into the category of wildflowers; more often they have actually been planted along country roadsides or flanking farm entrances, where the big clumps of floppy, channelled leaves are strong enough to cope with competition from tall grasses. In late summer, the flower stalks stand head-high with the tubular flower buds glowing red at the pointed end of the poker. By the time the flowers are properly open they have turned yellow, and hang pendulous on the lower part of the inflorescence.

Red hot pokers, *Kniphofia uvaria*, near Balclutha.

Another hardy member of the lily family, often naturalised on dry roadside banks, is *Agapanthus*, or, if you are into nicknames, Aggie's pants, or just Aggies. There are lots of names for this thing. Nile lily if you like, despite its origin not from the Nile end of Africa, but from the south, where they also call it bloulelie. Deep blue it usually is, though paler blue and white cultivars also occur, the flowers held in spherical bunches above tufts of arching strap-shaped leaves.

You don't have to be a big tall plant to cope with growing amongst rank grasses. In pastures or lawns, and along road verges of wet districts you might find one of the South American species of *Sisyrinchium*, at least four of which occur in New Zealand. Pale blue, striped or yellow flowers will show up, even though you may need to look twice to distinguish the grass-like foliage. Botanists are not quite sure of the correct names for all the weedy introduced "sissys". The one in the photo does not exactly match the descriptions in any overseas Floras, so it goes under the tag name of *Sisyrinchium* "blue".

Irises are well-known to gardeners as having some members which prefer dry ground, and others the wettest of wet. Yellow flag is an iris which will even grow standing in the water of a swamp or lake edge. You can see it beside the Rotorua lakes, or fringing Lake Rotoroa (Hamilton Lake) where it grows among raupo, and flies its yellow flags at about waist-height above tufts of spear-shaped leaves. In Christchurch, along the banks of the lower Avon and Heathcote Rivers,

Nile lily or Aggie's pants, *Agapanthus praecox* subsp. *orientalis*, at Napier.

Sisyrinchium "blue", Taramakau Valley, Westland.

there are populations with either pale or dark yellow flowers. In his book *Modern Nature*, Derek Jarman tells us that the yellow flag is "... known also as Jacob's sword, the flower with which he fought the angel. The flag is fleur-de-lis, flower of Saint Louis, the emblem of the Crusaders, the lily of France."

Stinking iris (likewise the name *Iris foetidissima*, meaning most smelly, and it is the whole plant which seems to smell), grows best in partial shade under trees, such as in cemeteries, old farm gardens, or in woodland such as that which flanks the side of Mt Eden, the hill, in Auckland city. A knee-high plant, with fans of floppy sword-shaped leaves, it is the leaves which smell unpleasant when bruised. The flowers you would scarcely notice, being not highly coloured, though they are beautifully and delicately veined. Stinking iris puts on a much better display of colour when in fruit, the opened capsules showing off rows of orange seeds.

Kaffir lily, despite its lily name, is also in the iris family. The seeds float along waterways, and in its native South Africa it is also known as river lily. In parts of Canterbury, Westland, and Southland during autumn, I have come across scarlet rows of flowering plants which follow the margins of roadside drains. In New Plymouth I have seen it beside river pools, doubling its display by the reflections.

Yellow flag, *Iris pseudacorus*, near Dunedin.

Stinking iris,
Iris foetidissima,
Dunedin.

Stinking iris in fruit.

Kaffir lily, *Schizostylis coccinea*,
in a roadside ditch, at Waituna
near Invercargill.

36 *Save Manapouri*

Fiordland (or if you like, Fairyland, because it is that sometimes), is more than just the fiords of its saltwater coast. It has the freshwater equivalent in the long, glacier-gouged arms of its major east side lakes, Te Anau, Manapouri, Monowai, Hauroko, Poteriteri. In total their shores are several hundred kilometres and it is not without the odd wet arse and the occasional fright, that I have travelled them all by dinghy. These lakes have disparate moods: ecstatically idyllic; over-poweringly sullen; unforgivingly nasty.

While safety in a small boat may not be assured by befriending the gods, it is nice to think they are on your side, or at least aware of your presence, insignificance, and vulnerability. I see it as important to pay my respects in various ways to the lakes, their spirits, their creations, their former and their present inhabitants.

Lake Manapouri, viewed from the prominent hill called The Monument.

Lake Manapouri, a sheltered turfy bay in Hope Arm, at a time of low lake level.

Lake Monowai, drowned beech trees on the shore.

Lake Manapouri: a sheltered turfy bay where today's visible inhabitants have included a not-very-scary hind and her yearling, a lazy eel, and a rainbow trout, cruising its beat, and rising casually to take surface morsels. Bubbles of marsh gas break the surface too, suppurating from leaf litter on the lake bed. Can I blame the marsh gas for a rare and unwanted headache which forces me, for shade relief, to rest beneath the edge of the manuka scrub? Hoverflies and blowflies check me out. Sandflies bite and bother me. Bird song comes and goes: I am treated to the morning calls, in live broadcast, of bellbird, blackbird, brown creeper, kakariki, rifleman, tomtit, grey warbler, and both sorts of cuckoo. I share the ground with a confetti of manuka petals. How odd that one flower should drop a spent petal just as I stare at it.

Twenty five years ago this corner of Fairyland was in the news, the subject of great debate as to whether the lake level should be raised, the shore forests flooded, the small islands drowned, in order to squeeze an extra bit more electricity from the hydro system. But the Save Manapouri Campaign worked. Thank goodness THEY didn't raise the lake. So far, the lake and the power station are still owned by us, the people. Let us not allow any future government to forget the effectiveness of a big petition and a public outcry.

Lake Monowai has been regarded as the ugly sister of the Fiordland lakes because of the fringe of dead trees, killed when the lake level was raised in 1926 for hydro-electricity. The shore is now partly healed, and anyway the remnant trunks and root plates have a beauty of their own. There is beauty too in some of the weeds that have invaded the marshy shore. Spearwort is an introduced buttercup with super-shiny yellow flowers. Here is a plant that can fool the unwary. The common name spearwort and the species name *flammula* (flame) both refer to the leaf shape, but depending on age, shade, and soil fertility, the leaves of this plant can vary from narrow to oval, and from long-stalked to stalkless.

Opposite page: Spearwort, *Ranunculus flammula*, at Lake Monowai.

Lake-edge turf

On gentle shores where silt accumulates, the rise and fall of Lake Manapouri plays upon a compact turf, studded with flowers in the summer months. This is nature's version of a bowling green. Most players of bowls or croquet will have walked and played on some of these lake edge plants and will know cotula, starweed, and pratia in their cultivated setting.

On a bowling green these tough little turfies will tolerate being walked upon, rolled flat, mown to almost skin-head degree, and to being thoroughly soaked. And no wonder: on lake shores they have become adapted to wave-action, partial burial by sediments, flooding, and to being grazed and shat on by water birds. Studying these tiny tufted or creeping herbs is the ultimate in hands-and-knees botany – wet knees at that. Most of the plants have leaves that are either linear, pinnatifid, or spathulate in shape, so I call them the "knife-fork-and-spoon" plants.

The photos show only 8 of at least 90 native species found on the turfy shores of Manapouri. It is the sort of rich habitat where new things turn up. I discovered an annual, white flowered cress, which fitted no described species, or even genus. In formally naming it we sought the shortest name that botanical Latin would allow, just three letters, and called the genus Iti, *from the Maori for diminutive, and the species* lacustris, *meaning lake shore.*

Not all of these lake edge plants had common names, so I have made some of them up. Bumbles (Hypsela rivalis) *has a rather ill-defined leaf shape, stems which bumble along the ground surface, and masses of starry white or bluish flowers which attract bumble bees. On some sunny days there can be so many bumble bees that you have to be careful not to walk on them in bare feet.*

The pink boys in Neopaxia *are the pink anthers, displayed against the white petals. You might hardly notice this plant when not in flower. The leaves are small, strap-shaped and nondescript. A closer look at different populations in their*

1. Bumbles, *Hypsela rivalis.*
2. Pink boys, *Neopaxia australasica.*
3. Selliera, *Selliera radicans.*
4. Flicks, *Glossostigma elatinoides.*

many distinct habitats suggests that this variable entity actually comprises several species.

The plant I call flicks is a great source of fun, because it will move when prodded in the right place. Flicks has paired, paddle-shaped leaves and grows as an aquatic in shallow water. When lakes are low, plants exposed to the air will open their tiny pinkish or purple flowers, and display the tongue-shaped stigma for which the genus Glossostigma is named. Botanists describe the stigma as "irritable". Touch the arching stigma lightly and it flicks up to an erect position, exposing the anthers beneath. After a few minutes the stigma returns to its original position, and is ready to perform again, in response to either a pollinating insect or an irritating observer.

Selliera has spoon-shaped, fleshy leaves and one-sided white flowers, like half stars. Although it grows in the upper zone of turf on some freshwater lakes, it is more characteristic of estuarine salt marshes on the sea coast.

The tubular flower bud of shorebright is red-striped but the flowers open white and are reminiscent of the alpine eyebrights (Euphrasia; see p.166) which likewise belong in the foxglove family.

Bladderwort flowers are usually purple with a yellow eye, or rarely whitish in some individuals. Bladderwort gets its name from the intricate bladders borne on underground stems, each one furnished with a frilly-edged trapdoor, designed to trap water fleas and other tiny animals that are then digested by the plant as an additional source of nutrients. This is of particular benefit when the plant is growing in puddly places of infertile peat bogs. The name Utricularia comes from utricula, a little bottle.

Pale pincushion is another plant which grows in bogs as well as lake shores, making bristly cushions, up to fist-size. Its little flash of colour comes from the red of the stigmas. In mini-milfoil it is the red anthers which provide the flower display, there being no showy petals. The other native milfoil species are larger plants, aquatics with mainly feathery leaves.

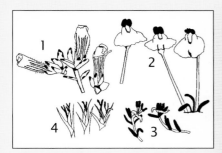

1. Shorebright,
   Gratiola sexdentata.
2. Bladderwort,
   Utricularia novae-zelandiae.
3. Mini-milfoil,
   Myriophyllum votschii.
4. Pale pincushion,
   Centrolepis pallida.

Red mistletoe, *Peraxilla colensoi*, growing on a silver beech tree, Eglinton Valley.

37

More of Fiordland

There are not many roads in Fiordland, which in our age of the car is an amazingly valuable thing, but you can drive yourself to Milford Sound, literally through Fiordland, within deep steep valleys, and via the Homer Tunnel.

On the way, if you stop in the Eglinton Valley you will find clumps of mistletoe, including the broad-leaved *Peraxilla colensoi*, growing upon the beech trees. Around New Year is a good time to see the best show of red flowers. Mistletoes are semi-parasites, gaining all their water and nutrients via modified roots which enter the stems or trunks of host trees or shrubs, yet having green leaves with which to manufacture their own food.

Several native mistletoes seem to be declining in abundance, and possum browsing has long been implicated as one of the causes. But recent research has pointed the finger also to the dwindling numbers of native honey-eater birds, especially tuis and bellbirds which know the trick of twisting open the ripe flower buds to gain access to nectar, as well as effecting pollination and ensuring seed set. Alas, this seems to be yet another flow-on effect that introduced predators such as rats, stoats, ferrets, and cats have had upon old New Zealand. Indeed, even throughout remote and seemingly pristine Fiordland, these seldom-seen predators are widespread and plentiful, leaving forests with flowers but with few birds to visit them.

One of our saddest birds must be the kakapo, beautiful green ground parrot of the night. Fiordland was the last mainland stronghold for kakapo, until a decade or so ago, and I was once lucky enough to see one of them, and to say goodnight to it, a lone male booming from his bowl in Sinbad Gully. In the classic view from the head of Milford Sound, the Sinbad is the U-shaped valley to the left of Mitre Peak. When you look up this valley to its steep head-wall, spare a thought,

Montbretia, *Crocosmia* ×*crocosmiiflora*, and the view to
Sinbad Gully and Mitre Peak from the head of Milford
Sound.

as I do, for those last few of a lost kakapo tribe, those
feathered gardeners who once had intricate systems
of manicured tracks all through this country.

Once on a visit to Milford I was struck by the
irony of a tourist visitor to this most green and rugged
of National Parks, concentrating her photography
on the orange flowers of montbretia, a cheap garden
discard. Years later I decided to overcome my own
purist prejudices by juxtaposing the pretty weed with
the beautiful Milford postcard scene. Nowadays you
might have trouble finding much montbretia here;
Department of Conservation workers have managed
to get rid of most of it. Its botanical name *Crocosmia*
×*crocosmiiflora* has the × preceding the species name
to indicate that it is a named artificial hybrid, in this
case between two South African species, *C. aurea*
and *C. pottsii*.

Montbretia can be a damnable plant to get rid of
from the garden. Regardless of the care taken to dig
it out you will always overlook some of the spherical
corms which occur in multiple stacks upon the
underground stems. Montbretia at Milford Sound
is probably a hangover from the earliest hotel garden.

The Fiordland coast and the many islands
at the entrance to Dusky Sound.

White flowers, black fruits

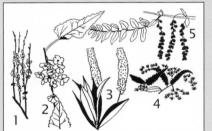

1. A native broom, *Carmichaelia grandiflora*.
2. Mountain ribbonwood, *Hoheria lyallii*.
3. Willow-leaved koromiko, *Hebe salicifolia* (the foliage like that of *Salix*, the willows).
4. Mountain holly, *Olearia ilicifolia* (the foliage like *Ilex*, holly).
5. Tutu, *Coriaria sarmentosa*.

These are plants of subalpine scrub, a zone of vegetation most colourful in its foliage, and in the harrowing stories of scrub-bashing by trampers and climbers. It is a zone of vegetation which gets bashed in the regular course of events by avalanche, rock-fall, and snow-lie. The photograph was taken in the upper Hollyford Valley, not far from Homer Tunnel, where the road is regularly closed in winter and spring because of snow and avalanche danger.

Mountain ribbonwood is a small tree, one of the few natives having deciduous leaves. The other plants are all shrubs. They illustrate the white flowers that are the norm in the New Zealand flora.

All the species of koromiko (Hebe) have opposite leaves, the young ones fused by their margins when in bud, each pair enclosing a progressively smaller pair towards the stem apex, like Russian dolls, one within the next within the next. Soft leafy tips of koromiko are a cure for dysentery.

Do not ever be tempted, in sickness or in health, by those purple-black fruits on tutu, for their poison, tutin, would leave you with more than a runny tummy. With care, an edible jam or jelly can be made from the fleshy part of the fruits, provided the seeds are excluded. Birds avoid being poisoned by eating the fruits whole and not retaining them in the gut for long enough for the seeds to be digested. Tutu foliage is also poisonous, indeed it has even been known to kill circus elephants that were travelling on foot from one New Zealand town to another, between performances. No such poisonings are known from Fiordland, and there is no suggestion that Hannibal ever passed by these mountains.

Fiordland coast

1. Shore gentian, *Gentiana saxosa*.
2. *Pimelea gnidia*.
3. Teteaweka, *Olearia oporina*.
4. Shore koromiko, *Hebe elliptica*.

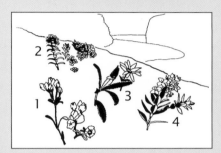

Just as we saw white flowers in the last bunch, from subalpine scrub, so we see white again in the native flowers of the Fiordland coast, including further representatives of the large genera Hebe *and* Olearia. *Whereas the subalpine plants have snow and avalanche to contend with, these coastal plants, upon a rocky shore at the entrance to Breaksea Sound, specialise in withstanding the onslaughts of coastal storms. As if not entirely happy with pure whiteness, shore koromiko sometimes have blue flowers. Teteaweka flower heads are constantly white in the rays but the central disc switches from yellow, as in this population, towards purple as you move south around the coast and to Stewart Island.* Pimelea gnidia *is a shrub that looks deceptively like a* Hebe *until you see its furry, daphne-like flowers, white or sometimes rose-coloured. Shore gentian is always white, but we shall see a brightly coloured subantarctic relative, before long.*

38 *Bluff – End of the Road*

New Zealanders who achieve a lasting place in the memories of fellow and later countryfolk are mostly sports heroes, war medallists, prison escapers. How easily, by contrast, we forget the names and faces of fleeting celebrities, most politicians, and television personalities.

One form of publicity stunt or pilgrimage that our long narrow country provides is the walk, or trek, or ride from North Cape to the Bluff. There are very few brownie points to be gained in doing it by car.

One well-known New Zealander, the publisher A.H. Reed, did this walk at age 85. I recall it because he came to address our school assembly. How much speaking time was allotted to him, who knows, but after forty minutes, when the story was no further south than Hamilton, the headmaster got up and stopped him. Yet this glimpse of A.H. Reed's enthusiasm, his gangly old frame, and his display of the very socks he had worn on the journey, are remembered while all those hundreds of other school assemblies are forgotten, thankfully.

As it happens, North Cape is not the northernmost point of New Zealand, nor is Bluff the southernmost, but they are near enough to being the top and bottom ends of State Highway 1. One wild plant linking these two ends of the country is Cape honey flower. In Northland it has colonised many sand-dunes, and at Bluff it covers a coastal slope, framing the harbour entrance and the incoming oyster boats, the reddish flower stalks matching the colour of the strange

Cape honey flower, *Melianthus major*, oyster boat and lighthouse at Bluff.

pimple-headed lighthouse. Cape honey flower is a *Melianthus* (from *meli* = honey and *anthos* = flower). *Melianthus major*. I like the name spoken aloud, and I especially like the pale bluish-green foliage, with serrated leaflets as if they had been cut out with pinking shears. It is a thicket-forming shrub with long angling stems, reddish-brown flowers that are loaded with nectar (ask any bellbird), and bladder-like fruits.

Bluff takes its name from the promontory hill that rises behind the town: The Bluff, appearing from out at sea as a dark land-

Cape honey flower on the dunes at Matai Bay, Northland.

mark, rising above a grey horizon and between squall clouds. You can drive to a lookout at the top of The Bluff and get a taste of the salty gales that sweep in from Foveaux Strait, and catch a whiff of the peaty soils to transport yourself across to Stewart Island.

Nice-looking dump

The end of the road for many of our belongings is the dump or rubbish tip. Maybe your local authority operates one under the title of "refuse disposal site", "transfer station" or "sanitary landfill", euphemisms that all amount to much the same thing. Sometimes my job takes me to the tip, usually to help with a revegetation scheme. Like many tips, the one at Invercargill has filled part of an estuary. This photo was taken in a wet hollow, where the ground was made of plastic bags, milk cartons, and sawdust, and the vegetation was all these pretty flowers.

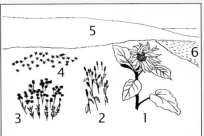

1. Sunflower, *Helianthus annuus*.
2. Willow weed, *Polygonum persicaria*.
3. Wild turnip, *Brassica rapa*.
4. Scentless mayweed, *Tripleurospermum inodorum*.
5. Sawdust, mostly *Pinus radiata*.
6. Milk cartons, also mostly *Pinus radiata*.

39 *Stewart Island*

As an abstraction, "island" has a Stewart Island origin for me, and my concept of "island time" derives from there also. One of the things I like about Stewart Island is that we do not use a car there, so that land travel is by walking the few kilometres of available roads and the many more of bush and boardwalk tracks. By going everywhere on foot, time and space seem to resume their proper relationship. There we have it: TIME again; that which is infinite in the big picture, yet exhaustible by each of us.

Another simple fascination of islands is their neat geographical definition, by water, which somehow confers a comfortable feeling of containment and belonging, as well as two exploratory challenges: circumnavigation and an ascent to the highest point.

Firstly: circumnavigation of Stewart Island. I have achieved this once, clockwise, as a passenger on *The Portland*, an old scow capable of about 6 knots, or a bit more with the sails up. Passing well out from South Cape we somehow misjudged position or timing of tidal current and were reduced to an effective speed of about 1 knot. How different it was a few days later when we passed through the confines of the Ruggedy Passage: it felt as if we were hitting 20 knots as we surged past rocky cliffs, tantalisingly close to the untouchable coastal flora.

Teteaweka, *Olearia oporina*, on Poutama, one of the Mutton Bird Islands.

Going ashore to botanise on southern coasts has its own quota of risks and rewards. Among the risks are some of the less-than-cute wildlife. Bull fur seals who wish to demonstrate their ownership of rock platforms and boulder beaches. Southern skuas which dive out of the sun to scrape claws across your head. My devised defence against these birds has been to carry a dead branch, upright so the branchlets protrude above scalp level, the stem held with upper arm against the body, allowing two hands free for notebook and pencil, and peace-of-mind against these sky-diving, shore-patrolling, predatory bandits.

Most dead branches on southern shores are likely to come from one of the tree-daisies, such as teteaweka, a stiffly-branched shrub with foliage tufts resembling miniature pineapple plants, and seen in the photo with a purple-centred flower head, contrasting with the yellow form we saw on the Fiordland coast (p. 147).

Seaside rock crevices and coastal tussock grasslands may not be where you would expect to find a forget-me-not, but this is the habitat of *Myosotis rakiura*.

Acaena anserinifolia, one of the bidibids,
at Ringaringa Beach.

Stewart Island forget-me-not, *Myosotis rakiura*, among coastal cliff tussocks, Solander Island.

Secondly: a complete ascent to Mt Anglem, the highest point of Stewart Island, has eluded me so far. My sons and I once tramped as far as the summit ridge, to be turned back by a hypothermia threat of rain and wind. We were sent scuttling back down the muddy track to Christmas Village hut, where the boys got the stove going to perfection, and I used the shelter of the forest to photograph lantern-berries. A little wiry herb, found on mossy fallen logs or tree buttresses, lantern-berry has a crisp white flower, which hangs like that of a snowdrop or snowflake (see p. 23) and is similarly green-veined inside, when viewed from beneath. The fleshy berries, also white and opaque, persist on the plants for many months, so you often find the flowers of one season alongside berries from the last.

Trampers and walkers on Stewart Island, as elsewhere in New Zealand, are likely to encounter one or more species of *Acaena*, the bidibids or piripiri. What could be nicer, to the ear, than piripiri at Ringaringa, or conversely worse, to the temperament, than getting all those burs stuck in your socks?

Lantern-berry or nohi, *Luzuriaga parviflora*,
on a mossy forest floor.

Obbsy Bobbsy Rock

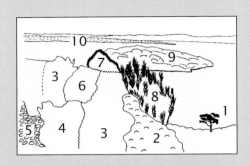

1. Rimu, *Dacrydium cupressinum*.
2. Muttonbird scrub, *Brachyglottis rotundifolia*.
3. Kamahi, *Weinmannia racemosa*.
4. Stinkwood, *Coprosma foetidissima*.
5. Broadleaf, *Griselinia littoralis*.
6. Shining karamu, *Coprosma lucida*.
7. Southern rata, *Metrosideros umbellata*.
8. Inaka or turpentine scrub, *Dracophyllum longifolium*.
9. Iona Island.
10. Ulva Island.

All my visits to Rakiura – this green heap of island with glowing skies – have included a walk to Observation Rock, up behind the township of Halfmoon Bay. It is partly a nostalgic walk, with recollections of our mother taking David and me (aged 4 and 6) on our first Stewart Island holiday. My little notebook diary again, with its sellotaped photos: 22.5.1953 "In the morning we climbed up to Obbsy Bobbsy rock. Then we went down to Golden Bay and threw stones at the octopuses."

The hilltop view from Observation Rock helps to explain the layout of inlets and islets, and allows you to rub noses with a natural arrangement of the common trees and shrubs. This collection of plants – the least contrived bunch in the book – does not exhibit any flowers, nor, I admit, does the picture show diagnostic features of leaves that would clinch identification of each item. But then again, our recognition of different plants is often based upon distant views of subtle characters such as plant posture, architecture, or the texture and colour of foliage.

That silhouetted tree I know to be a rimu, not from having checked its rippling bark plates, nor its whipcord foliage fallen from the crown, nor from any comparison of its wood with the rimu timber familiar on the carpentry bench. Confident recognition must stem, I guess, from having seen thousands of rimu trees in passing, including contorted windshorn ones with their crowns steadfastly held above the general level of the coastal canopy.

Muttonbird scrub I can recognise in the photo by the flash of white leaf undersides. Any visitor to Stewart Island could identify this plant by its leathery leaf, almost round in outline. You can write on the furry white side of the leaf; alas, the postal authorities no longer accept the naked leaf, postage stamp notwithstanding, as a stand-alone Stewart Island postcard.

A uniquely Rakiura mix

I'll wager that there is nowhere in the world other than Rakiura – Stewart Island – where these five plants grow wild together. None of them is native to the island, indeed the only New Zealander, the tainui, is classified as a threatened plant, now known as natural populations only at two sites in North Taranaki, although it occurs also in Australia. Here on Rakiura, along the road which fringes Halfmoon Bay, tainui has escaped from cultivation, onto sunny banks of rotten granite.

Past the little scimitar of beach called Lonnekers, with its line of heavy black sand and its strand of gum nuts, the road rises above the boatsheds and dinghies, and along an airy avenue of bluegums, their flowers providing nectar fuel for the tuis up high, to lubricate their lyrics and energise their rushes of flight.

By jumping up to grab a lower branch it is possible to catch some bluegum flowers, and discover what the tui no doubt has often seen: the flower bud at the clownish stage when its lid – knobbly, crinkled, and circumscissile – is pushed off by the expanding fuzzy-wuzzy head of white stamens. The botanist L'Héretier was also struck by this lid covering the flower bud when, in 1788, he coined

1. Tainui, *Pomaderris apetala*, from the North Island.
2. Red escallonia, *Escallonia rubra*, from Chile.
3. English honeysuckle, *Lonicera periclymenum*, from England, Europe, North Africa.
4. Balm of Gilead, *Cedronella canariensis*, from Madeira and the Canary Islands.
5. Tasmanian bluegum, *Eucalyptus globulus*, from Tasmania.

40 *A Bunch of Wild Orchids*

the name Eucalyptus *from the Greek* eu = well, *and* kalyptos = covered. *Poor old L'Héretier was murdered mysteriously, run through with a sabre in the street. Dangerous game, botany!*

Ah, the smell of gum nuts or crushed young eucalypt leaves, to take us on to Leasks Bay, (where I once caught a conger eel as long as myself – we were both 5 ft) and where the other hand, untainted (back to the present story), can be used to crush the Balm of Gilead shrub for its smell, or to pick a fragrant honeysuckle or a sticky-stemmed red escallonia, hedge plant gone wild.

One of those well-timed presents for a childhood Christmas at Stewart Island was *A Bunch of Wild Orchids* by Sheila Natusch, a delightful little book about the orchids which surrounded her upbringing on the island. My baseline of orchid enthusiasm was laid by this combination of book, summer holiday, and Stewart Island.

There is a universal magic about orchids, and several features help to explain their captivating influence. For one thing the orchid family is huge, with at least 20,000 species worldwide. About 130 orchids are native to New Zealand, and the mere 30 which reach Stewart Island are still a sufficient number to challenge the observer.

Most orchids are scattered in their distribution and often only seasonally obvious, so there is always an element of surprise in making an encounter. There

Lady's slipper orchid, *Dendrobium cunninghamii*, catches the early morning sun on the coastal bush edge at Port William, Stewart Island.

are ones just frequent enough to capture a beginner's interest, others chanced upon in the right season in bush or bog or on a clay bank, some almost extinct or which from time to time are rediscovered, and more besides which are as yet unnamed. Orchids are Nature's ornamentals, rather than Earth's vegetation. They may be plain in their foliage, but in the evolution of their flowers they have played fantastic tricks with form and colour to ensure the "cooperation" of specific pollinating insects.

At Stewart Island we stay in a hut, linked by a short bush track to the cemetery. It is close enough to take a breakfast mug of tea or evening cup of coffee, and to sit among orchids as well as among the departed, on a grassy spur. The outlook is a gentle one over a little bay with golden sand and soft waves, past bush headlands towards mummified islands out to sea.

I write this sitting beside the mound of a departed acquaintance. It is said that Max Kershaw took to his grave secrets of rare birds. In the lawn beside him are not-so-rare onion orchids, happily competing with the introduced grasses and clovers, oxeye daisies and plantains, and coping with occasional beheading at mowing time.

Orchids seem to interweave among the bods in this bush-clearing cemetery. On Eric Leask's headstone is an engraved picture of his boat the *Olga*, seen in a view from the shore through a curtain of Easter orchids. I remember Mr Leask and the *Olga* from trips to Paterson Inlet, to coves with water so clear that you could see the blue cod on the bottom, and islands where the bush orchids grew. I was allowed a turn at the tiller too, and got the feel of holding a heading while we sailed the length of the inlet with a lively westerly aft. I remember Alfie Leask too, not for orchid connections, but because when we were kids fishing together on the wharf, his way of keeping his jeans looking clean was to wear them inside-out once the outside was dirty. Now I see that he and his sister are both in the same cemetery as their grandfather, having drowned at sea, somewhere round the south-west coast, maybe near one of those titi islands where sun orchids in the hilltop pakihi bogs open their purple flowers on those days that have a long enough burst of sunshine.

Greenhood orchids grow on the ground in the bush just below the cemetery. Just as the sea lures

Onion orchid, *Microtis unifolia*, Stewart Island.

Greenhood orchids, *Pterostylis banksii*, Stewart Island.

Opposite page: Easter orchid or raupeka, *Earina autumnalis*, from near Dunedin.

fisherfolk with its attractions and its dangers, greenhood orchids can dish up rough treatment to the insects lured into their flowery caverns. How odd it seems for a flower to be green, to not have a colour that contrasts with the foliage. In fact, these greenhood orchids do make their play with a splash of dull redness on the tapered tips of "beak" and "horns", and nor is the rest of the flower just plain green. The hood contains transparent segments that appear white from the outside. From within, these appear like tall windows at the end of a cathedral, which glisten like frosted glass when struck by the dappled light that reaches the forest floor. At the

Spider orchid, *Corybas macranthus*, Silverstream near Dunedin.

entrance to the inner sanctum is a black-edged tongue, a landing pad for insects, yet at the same time a trapdoor, trigger-sensitive to touch, which hurls the insect into the bowels of the flower. Escape is then possible only by climbing and squeezing past sticky stigma, and then past sticky stamen.

Spider orchids are among the most beautiful plants that I know. The foliage is utterly simple: just a single plate-like leaf, flat and fleshy, fresh salad green above, but the underside silvery white from the huge numbers of stomata or breathing pores. The flower is much more ornate. It has a cap-like roof with a long peak to keep the rain off, a watery-transparent texture but flecked with rich purple. From the inside, with backlighting, it is like stained glass. Insects must enter the cave-like flower by climbing the wide sloping apron of the front floor. At the back of the cave the purpleness deepens, except for a pale beckoning rib down the back, down a crevasse where the insects get an enforced encounter with stamen and stigma and presumably exit through one of the pair of flared nostril openings at the flower base.

The spider orchid has a smell, not obvious at first, but very clingy to my fingers after handling and dissecting a flower. A fragrant pong that reminds me of some other bush smell; I am not sure what.

My favourite orchid smell is that of Easter orchid, a sweet almost syrupy smell which wafts from small white flowers perched upon forest trees or logs or rocks. Fiordland boat skipper Lance Shaw has told me that on a fine autumn day you can be right out in the middle of one of the fiords and still catch the Easter orchid smell drifting out from one of the forested shores.

Lady's slipper orchid is another widespread perching orchid, producing tufts or dangles of brittle stems, like very thin bamboo, and with summer flowers, which lack fragrance. The name lady's slipper comes from the distinctive shape of the flower bud.

Lady's slipper orchid, *Dendrobium cunninghamii*.

41

Flowers on Trees

Tree fuchsia, kotukutuku, *Fuchsia excorticata*, Taramakau Valley, Westland.

Cabbage tree, ti, *Cordyline australis*, near Kyeburn, Central Otago.

For a large part of my childhood I was a forest dweller, in the bush of the Dunedin Town Belt, a place for tree or underground huts, gang fights and other forms of territorial behaviour, bike tracks, bird watching, and nature study of one sort or another. The Town Belt was also a source of many useful items which today would be termed natural resources or indigenous heritage, depending upon which euphemistic side of the fence you sit on. In childhood we harvested the raw materials in our patch, as of right, though not necessarily without guilt (as experienced after "accidentally" scoring a hit on a wood pigeon), nor without surreptitiousness (as in hiding the evidence of a felled sapling). We learned, first-hand, about environmental impacts, and about which plants were capable of recovery, and at what rates.

One of the flowering trees to become a friend for life was the native tree fuchsia, largest fuchsia in the world so the books said, larger than any of the more numerous species in South America, original home of most of the garden fuchsias. The flowers of trees are not always obvious or accessible, but those of tree fuchsia are an exception, many of them arising directly from the lower stems or even from the trunk. They are unusual also in having pollen that is both blue and sticky, often seen as face-paint on the otherwise green snouts of bellbirds.

Our tree fuchsia, the kotukutuku, gave us konini, the sweet fleshy purple berries full of tiny seeds. From the trunk we licked the sweet drops of sap which bled instantly from a cut made with a sharp pocket knife. Unfortunately, this infliction resulted in nasty weals for the healing tree (or semi-permanent initials for those who carved who-loves-whom messages). *Fuchsia* is named after a sixteenth century German botanist, Leonard Fuchs, who would no doubt be appalled to hear his plant pronounced "fewsha", as we all do. *Fuchsia excorticata* is named for the bark which so obviously excorticates – it peels off the wood – in orange-brown papery sheets. This was our stuff for bush cigarettes. All the kids could roll their own, though why we bothered I don't know, for fuchsia bark burned awfully hot, and it was a simple enough matter to buy the real thing. Many mothers were heavy smokers who kept an account at the dairy or the grocer. So for us, it was just "20 Players Plain for Mrs Sim please, on her account", or "10 Capstan Cork for Mrs Thomas".

Another flowering tree which we abused as kids was the cabbage tree, by chopping vertical lines of footholds up the soft trunks. I did not know then that one day I would be termed a conservationist, and despite having once read *The Water Babies* I did not then realise the aptness of Charles Kingsley's words, "He did not know that a keeper is only a poacher turned inside out, and a poacher a keeper turned inside out."

Cabbage trees are such a symbol of the New Zealand landscape that I recommend every suburban garden should have one, partly for

Left: Tarata or lemonwood, *Pittosporum eugenioides.*

Right: Kohuhu, *Pittosporum tenuifolium.*

Tarata and Kohuhu

As wild trees, these two crinkly-leaved pittosporums are common components of several types of native forest, and as garden subjects their flowers are a bonus on top of other good horticultural qualities. Tarata has an elegant whitish trunk and a rounded bushy crown of pale leaves with distinctive white midribs. A cultivar with variegated leaves has become popular, especially in Australian gardens, although it beats me why gardeners show such passion for variegated plants which are, in effect, mutated monstrosities. The name lemonwood would seem to derive from the lemon-like odour of the crushed leaves. The masses of yellow-green flowers are intensely sweet-smelling.

Kohuhu flowers are very different, dark purple to almost black, and they become odoriferous only by night when they are pollinated by moths. Kohuhu has smaller, thinner leaves than those of tarata, although they are variable in size, and we see a relatively large-leaved southern South Island form in this photo. Wild plants with much smaller leaves are the norm further north, and these have given rise to numerous garden cultivars.

the fragrant flowers, and partly with a more devious motive. The fibrous leaves of cabbage trees are awful things for getting wrapped around motor mowers. So if there were more front-garden cabbage trees, perhaps more people would give up on the fetish of lawn-mowing, and our suburbs would become a good deal quieter.

Cabbage trees hold their little white flowers in a massive panicle, too large and too far out-of-reach to pick for a vase, so the sweet smell must be enjoyed out in the open air, for which it was intended anyway. You wouldn't get much of a feed from the tiny fleshy berries, although the birds certainly do so. However, you could try keeping hunger at bay by roasting the apical bud of young leaves. Perhaps you might find it a less bitter experience than we did, as boy scouts, on a survival weekend.

It is perhaps as well that we did not have access to nikau palms at our end of the country, lest we might have tried to eat the "rich man's cabbage", the one and only apical shoot, without which a palm tree dies. On the New Zealand mainland we have just this one native palm, which reaches as far south as about Greymouth, Banks Peninsula, and

the Chatham Islands. The flowers of nikau appear on a bunch of tassels on the trunk, immediately beneath the lowest bulging leaf sheath. You need monkey or possum skills in order to see them up close, or else climb on the roof of your campervan, as I did with tripod and camera, hoping not to leave any dents noticeable to the hire company.

Nikau, *Rhopalostylis sapida*, the only palm tree native to the New Zealand mainland, at Kaihoka Lakes, Northwest Nelson.

The male flowers of nikau.

Thorny critters

A good way to get to know and perhaps to dislike these two barberries is to tackle an old hedge that needs removal, or to watch your farm or forest becoming infested with the spiny shrubs.

Berberis glaucocarpa was growing in our garden before we arrived, as a small tree displaying brilliant yellow wood and sawdust every time we pruned or felled it, and showing rapid spiny regrowth from the cut stumps. One year we thought the flowers looked pretty enough to pick, but what we also brought inside was the smell of chlorine. Thereafter we have called it "The Moana Pool Plant" after our local chlorinated swimming pool.

These two barberries originate from very different places – B. glaucocarpa from the western Himalayas and B. darwinii from southern Chile and Patagonia. The name glaucocarpa refers to the glaucous fruits: the bluish-grey colour produced in this case by a powdery coating which is easily rubbed off. A botanist might use the term pruinose for such a surface bloom, found also on many plums and grapes. The fruits of B. darwinii have the same feature.

The barberries are more than just prickly customers; they have trigger-happy flowers as well. The stamens are partly enclosed within the incurved petals, and when touched near the base of the filament they instantly bend inwards, then gradually relax again over a few minutes. The part to touch is the filament (or stalk) of the stamens.

Left: Darwin's barberry, *Berberis darwinii.*   Right: Barberry, *Berberis glaucocarpa.*

Kiwi icons

1. Manuka, a red-flowered cultivar, *Leptospermum scoparium*.
2. Kowhai, *Sophora microphylla*.
3. Pohutukawa, *Metrosideros excelsa*.
4. Puawhaananga, *Clematis paniculata*.

This is what I call the biscuit tin collection: a battered tin lid that made an appearance out on our roadside bank, with its crude paintings of well-known native bush plants. I found we were able to match all of them with sprigs from the garden.

42 *Away, Away Down South*

I guess we all have an interest in banknotes, yet we seldom look at them closely, just keep on pocketing them, keep on having to pass them on. Now, although the cache of banknotes on the Cairnmuir Range eluded me (see p. 128), I did once find the real quid further up the valley, in the scrub beside the Clutha River at Luggate Bridge. A great big pound note, the colour of purple linaria, lost in the scrub probably by some wealthy or careless angler. Finders keepers; his loss, my gain: many weeks' worth of pocket money.

Money, as we all know, equals spending power. Nevertheless there are some situations where hard currency is absolutely useless. For example, you are on a trip into the mountains or out at sea. You discover, among your gear, some coins or notes. You are days away – maybe going on light years – from any corner shop. The money loses its meaning. The coins become mere weight to be carried.

Despite this, I do know of one reason for taking banknotes with you on a far-south adventure. If you should head into Fiordland then there is a slim chance that the plant drawing on the $10 note will allow you to recognise the Fiordland form of *Parahebe catarractae*. You will get far better value for money by taking a $5 note to the subantarctic Campbell or Auckland Islands. This note depicts *Bulbinella rossii*, the largest of the yellow-flowered Maori onions, and *Pleurophyllum speciosum*, a daisy having bold, corrugated leaves and beautiful pink flower heads. The flower colour is not shown on the banknote; nor can I offer a picture to support my words for none of my photos do justice to this *speciosum* species.

Instead I shall attempt a very potted coverage of the subantarctic and its flowers, using just three pictures, taken at the Auckland Islands, and three

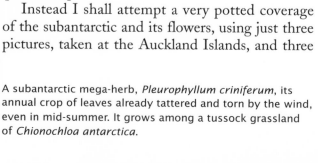

A subantarctic mega-herb, *Pleurophyllum criniferum*, its annual crop of leaves already tattered and torn by the wind, even in mid-summer. It grows among a tussock grassland of *Chionochloa antarctica*.

Flowering trees of southern rata, *Metrosideros umbellata*, on the windswept shores of Ross Harbour on subantarctic Auckland Island.

A red gentian, *Gentiana cerina*, growing no taller than the adjacent mosses and lichens, on top of Mt Dick, Auckland Islands.

keywords: weather, mega-herb, and colour.

The subantarctic Auckland Islands have such awful weather that you might wonder how any plants could manage to muster enough energy to flower and fruit in the face of such climatic tempest. Winds are strong and persistent. Temperature is constantly low. About 30 days of the year are free of a measurable amount of rainfall. There are even fewer days when cloud does not cover the hill crests. At this latitude − around 51 degrees south, forest can do no more than form a narrow fringe that hugs the more sheltered shores, yet this forest of southern rata still manages to produce masses of red flowers across the windshorn tree canopies.

The term "mega-herb" describes an assortment of huge-leaved, soft perennials, a growth form that seems incongruous in such a harsh climate, the more so because many of them are summer-green, and therefore must produce a whole new mass of foliage for each growing season. *Pleurophyllum criniferum* is one of the mega-herbs, having floppy white-backed leaves to 1 m long, and a tall stalk with globular heads that are purplish in flower, chocolate-brown in fruit.

Many plants from the subantarctic and Chatham Islands are renowned for having coloured flowers, in contrast to the white flowers of their mainland New Zealand relatives. Examples can be seen among daisies, the subantarctic carrots (*Anisotome*), a forget-me-not, and some gentians. The red gentian in the photo was an unexpected bonus when I crawled onto the top of Mt Dick, highest point (668 m) of the Auckland Islands. In shape, this is more of a large hill than a mountain and I was crawling not from any fear of falling down a steep slope, but because of the wind. During the climb, squalls with horizontal hail had dictated regular stops behind sheltering tussocks or rock out-crops. No such shelter was pro-vided on the summit ridge, hence my hands-and-knees stance, my hasty look at waterfalls that were blowing vertically upwards from the southern cliffs, and some snapshot photos, rapidly and roughly focused with watering eyes. What a place to be a flower!

43

What are Flowers for, Anyway?

False spaniard, *Celmisia lyallii* (with seedheads and spiky leaves); *Hebe hectorii* (whipcord foliage); *Gentiana corymbifera* (with the tussock butterfly, *Argyrophenga antipodum*); *Brachyglottis bellidioides* (yellow flowers); and eyebright, *Euphrasia zelandica,* at the bottom of the bunch; Coronet Peak, Otago.

Despite their appeal, their beauty, and their intricacy, flowers were never intended for our eyes, at least not in an evolutionary sense. For one thing flowers evolved long, long before humans were here to see them. The critical and remarkable fact is that flowers came about as a more efficient way for plants to share their genes. Interbreeding or cross-fertilisation has the benefit that it can mix the best of both parents, and selection, especially by the great hand of climate, may grant to the superior offspring, the gift of successful and proliferous life. Plants that have showy flowers are signalling, not to us, nor to each other, but mostly to insects, often to birds, sometimes to lizards and bats and other vertebrates. Using bright colours, fragrant smells, massed displays, intricate guidelines upon petals, and perfect timing, flowers are advertising food rewards of nectar and pollen to these mobile creatures. For their part, the pollinators are simply gathering resources, while being unwittingly manipulated into transferring pollen to stigmas, and hence being carriers of genes and hereditary information.

Evolution of flowering plants and of insects has happened together over millions of years. Our role as observers and admirers is a very recent one.

That flowers did not evolve for human eyes is supported by the knowledge that we do not perceive the full range of flower colours and patterns. Many insects have the ability to see additional colours in the UV range of light wavelengths. As an organism having reasonably good colour vision we humans should be grateful that the evolutionary selective influence of these pollinators would seem to have included an appreciation of form, proportion, and gradation of colour; in a nutshell: aesthetics.

And what comes after flowers?

... seeds, ... fruits, ... dried arrangements...

Wild fruits from Skippers

If you are in Queenstown and willing to tackle a slim, tortuous, hair-raising road, then head for Skippers and up towards Mt Aurum – the gold mountain. The route is perched above a gorged river full of rapids and boulders and sediment, a river which the gold miners called the Overshot, and which we now know as the Shotover. A number one river this, for commercial rafting, or you could bungy jump into its shady canyon from the awesome Skippers Bridge.

Alternatively, take a walk beyond Skippers Bridge, along the rough vehicle track towards the old hotel, through trees of sycamore and larch and Douglas fir that have spread from the cemetery, and make your own fruit salad collection of feral fruits. We made this collection in late February.

1. Blackberry, *Rubus fruticosus* aggregate.
2. Gooseberry, *Ribes uva-crispa*.
3. Strawberry, *Fragaria ✕ananassa*.
4. Raspberry, *Rubus idaeus*.

Autumn at Arrowtown

1. Elder, *Sambucus nigra*.
2. Rowan, *Sorbus aucuparia*.
3. Hawthorn, *Crataegus monogyna*.
4. Plums, *Prunus ✕domestica*.
5. Sycamore, *Acer pseudoplatanus*.
6. Bittersweet, *Solanum dulcamara*.

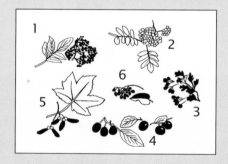

Arrowtown: an old gold-mining town beside the Arrow River, near Queenstown; a tourist drawcard especially when autumn leaves make coloured carpets beneath the town avenues, and up the hill flanks, and in the stream gullies where you can still see the autumn years of stone huts where the miners lived.

Autumn: where have all the flowers gone? The petals and the withered male parts will have gone already to life's great compost heap. The female parts of the flowers – demonstrating that a woman's work is never finished – will have moved on to the tasks of ripening seed and packaging it for transport.

Sycamore dresses its seeds with a wing like that of a miniature model aeroplane, and each seed goes for a single flying lesson: spinning. Elder, rowan, and bittersweet, are colourfully gift-wrapped to be avidly gobbled by birds. Hawthorn would appear to offer less tasty pickings, for in New Zealand most fruits remain on the trees until very late in the season, but this is probably because we lack large flocks of migratory birds to devour them. These plums are horticultural discards, bred to be larger than a comfortable beak-full for a bird. So they await a human hand, to guide them to the dessert bowl or the jam pan.

Cut and dried

Here we are at the very end of the flowering season, looking again at three plants we have seen earlier in the book and earlier in our journey. Yarrow flowers were in that kete in the frontispiece, and among the Six Common Daisies, and at Bannockburn. Honesty was flowering up the Leith, and I also showed you the "x-ray" photo of the seeds. What we see now are the innermost silvery membranes of the old dried capsules. Curled dock made a previous appearance, also in a somewhat seedy state on page 34. The one plant we have not seen before is teasel, an upright herb to 2 m tall, which grows in damp ground in sunny places. Its generic name Dipsacus derives from a Greek word for thirst, and the analogy may come from the pools of limpid water that gather in the cup-like leaf axils when the plant is green and actively growing. Late in the season teasel plants dry off to be brown and stiff, with prickly seed heads, once used to raise the nap on cloth. They are also of everlasting use in dried arrangements, for gathering dust and cobwebs, as they help to tide us over to another flowering season.

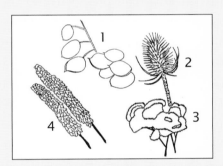

1. Honesty, *Lunaria annua*.
2. Wild teasel, *Dipsacus sylvestris*.
3. Yarrow, *Achillea millefolium*.
4. Curled dock, *Rumex crispus*.

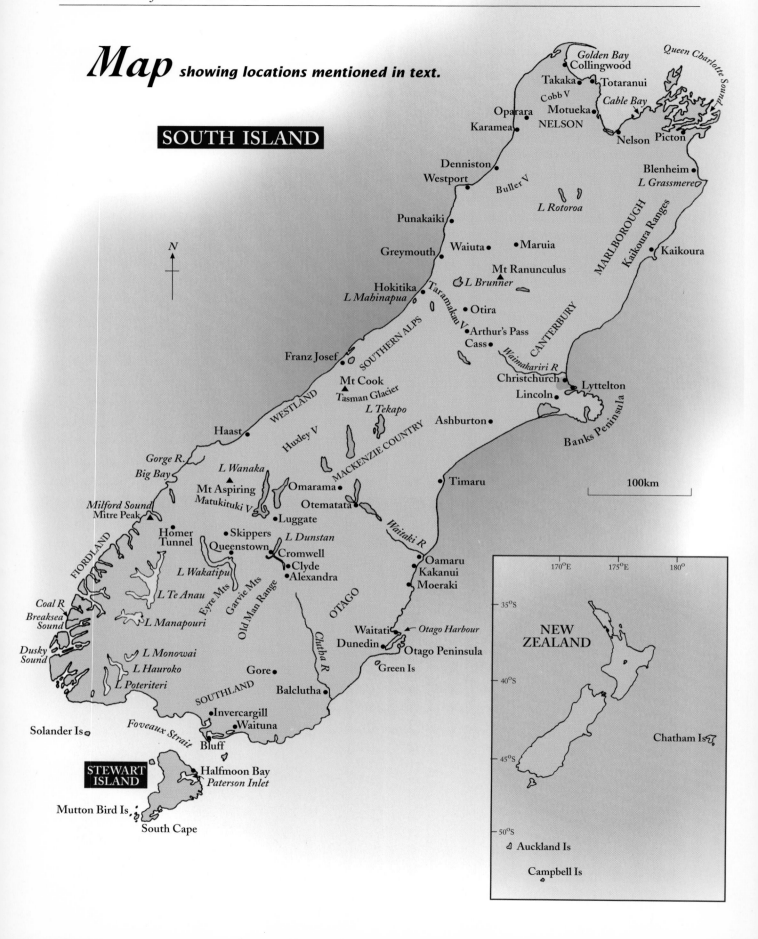

Map showing locations mentioned in text.

SOUTH ISLAND

N

100km

Golden Bay
Collingwood
Takaka
Totaranui
Cobb V
Cable Bay
Oparara
Motueka
Karamea
NELSON
Nelson
Picton
Queen Charlotte Sound

Denniston
Westport
Buller V
Blenheim
L Grassmere

Punakaiki
L Rotoroa

Waiuta
Maruia
Greymouth
Mt Ranunculus
Kaikoura
MARLBOROUGH
Kaikoura Ranges

Hokitika
L Mahinapua
Taramakau V
L Brunner
Otira
Arthur's Pass
Cass
CANTERBURY

Franz Josef
SOUTHERN ALPS
Waimakariri R

Mt Cook
Tasman Glacier
Christchurch
Lincoln
Lyttelton

WESTLAND
L Tekapo
Ashburton
Banks Peninsula

Haast
Huxley V
MACKENZIE COUNTRY

Gorge R.
Big Bay
L Wanaka
Omarama
Timaru

Mt Aspiring
Matukituki V
Otematata

Milford Sound
Mitre Peak
Luggate
Waitaki R

Homer
Tunnel
Skippers
L Dunstan
Oamaru
Kakanui
Moeraki

Queenstown
Cromwell
Clyde
Alexandra

FIORDLAND
L Wakatipu
Eyre Mts
Garvie Mts
Old Man Range
OTAGO

Coal R
Breaksea
Sound
L Te Anau

Dusky
Sound
L Manapouri
Waitati
Otago Harbour
Dunedin
Otago Peninsula

L Monowai
L Hauroko
Chatha R
Green Is

L Poteriteri
Gore

SOUTHLAND
Balclutha

Solander Is
Foveaux Strait
Invercargill
Waituna

Bluff

STEWART
ISLAND
Halfmoon Bay
Paterson Inlet

Mutton Bird Is
South Cape

170°E
175°E
180°

35°S
NEW
ZEALAND
40°S
45°S
Chatham Is
50°S

Auckland Is
Campbell Is

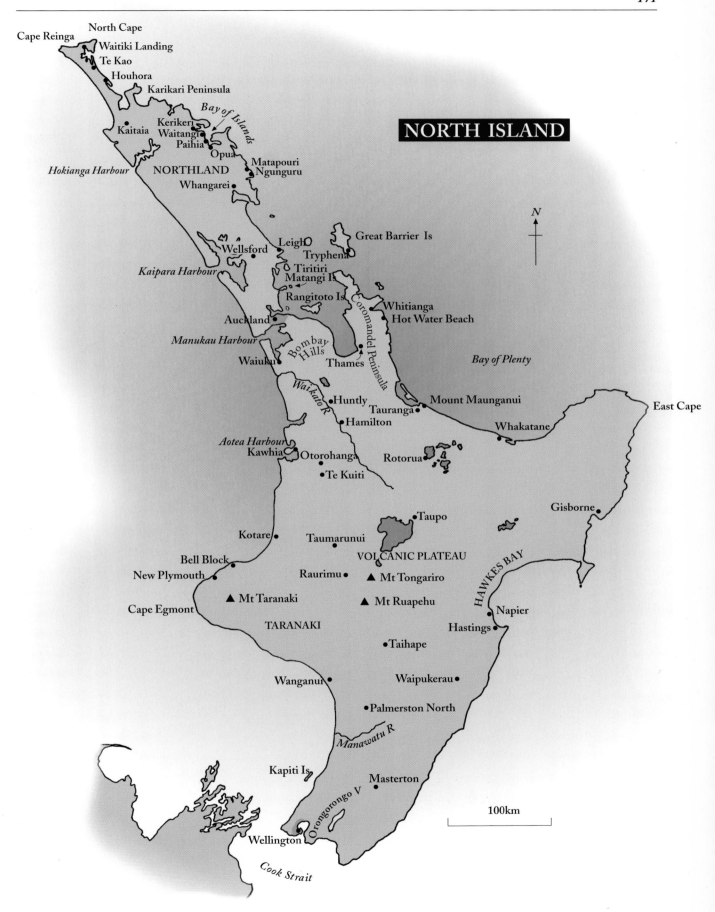

NORTH ISLAND

Cape Reinga
North Cape
Waitiki Landing
Te Kao
Houhora
Karikari Peninsula
Kaitaia
Kerikeri
Waitangi
Paihia
Opua
Bay of Islands
Matapouri
Ngunguru
NORTHLAND
Hokianga Harbour
Whangarei

Leigh
Great Barrier Is
Wellsford
Tryphena
Kaipara Harbour
Tiritiri
Matangi Is
Rangitoto Is
Whitianga
Hot Water Beach
Auckland
Coromandel Peninsula
Manukau Harbour
Bombay Hills
Bay of Plenty
Waiuku
Thames
Waikato R
Huntly
Mount Maunganui
East Cape
Tauranga
Hamilton
Whakatane
Aotea Harbour
Kawhia
Otorohanga
Rotorua
Te Kuiti

Gisborne

Taupo
Kotare
Taumarunui
VOLCANIC PLATEAU
Bell Block
Raurimu
▲ Mt Tongariro
New Plymouth
HAWKES BAY
Cape Egmont
▲ Mt Taranaki
▲ Mt Ruapehu
Napier
TARANAKI
Hastings
Taihape
Wanganui
Waipukerau
• Palmerston North
Manawatu R
Kapiti Is
Masterton
Orongorongo V
100km
Wellington
Cook Strait

N

Table Botanical and common names, families, places of origin, and flowering times.

Page numbers in **bold** indicate pictorial reference; plain numbers are text reference only.

Botanical names	Common names	Page	Family	Place of origin	Flowering months
A					
Acaena anserinifolia	bidibid	**151**	Rosaceae	N.Z.	11-1
Acer pseudoplatanus	sycamore	**168**	Aceraceae	C. & S. Europe	10-11
Achillea millefolium	yarrow	**6, 31, 130, 169**	Asteraceae	Europe, Caucasia, Iran, Siberia, Himalaya	(6)-12-5-(7)
Aeonium haworthii	pinwheel aeonium	**65**	Crassulaceae	Canary Is.	10-12-(2)
Aeonium undulatum	giant aeonium	**17**	Crassulaceae	Canary Is.	10-11-(12)
Agapanthus praecox subsp. *orientalis*	Nile lily	136, **137**	Alliaceae	S. Africa	12-4
Agave americana	century plant	**77**	Agavaceae	Mexico	1-3
Ageratina adenophora	Mexican devil	**87**	Asteraceae	Mexico	8-12-(3)
Ajuga reptans	bugle	**46**	Lamiaceae	temperate Eurasia, N. Africa	1-12
Allium triquetrum	onion weed	**23**	Alliaceae	S.W. Europe, N. Africa	(4)-6-11- (12)
Alocasia brisbanensis	elephant's ear	**99**	Araceae	Queensland	1-4
Aloe saponaria		**78**	Asphodelaceae	S. Africa	11-1
Alstroemeria aurea	Peruvian lily	69, **123**	Alstroemeriaceae	Argentina, Chile	12-2
Alternanthera philoxeroides	alligator weed	**88**	Amaranthaceae	Brazil	10-2
Ammophila arenaria	marram grass	**57, 60**	Poaceae	W. Europe, N. Africa	10-2
Anthemis cotula	stinking mayweed	**30**	Asteraceae	Europe, N. Africa, Caucasia to Iran, Iraq	(8)-12-3-(6)
Antirrhinum majus	snapdragon	**113**	Scrophulariaceae	S.W. Europe	1-12
Apium prostratum	native celery	**60**	Apiaceae	N.Z., also Australia, S. America, Pacific	10-4
Aponogeton distachyos	Cape pondweed	**123**	Aponogetonaceae	S. Africa	8-12-(7)
Aptenia cordifolia		**20**	Aizoaceae	S. Africa	1-12
Araujia sericifera	moth plant	**71**	Asclepiadaceae	Brazil, Argentina	12-5
Arctotheca calendula	Cape weed	**80**	Asteraceae	S. Africa	(8)-10-4
Argyranthemum frutescens	marguerite	**64, 65**	Asteraceae	Canary Is.	11-2-(10)
Aristea ecklonii	aristea	**93**	Iridaceae	W. & S. Africa	10-1
Arum italicum	Italian arum	**100**	Araceae	Europe	9-11
Asphodelus fistulosus	asphodel	**95**	Asphodelaceae	Mediterranean	7-11-(5)
B					
Barbarea intermedia	winter cress	**26**	Brassicaceae	Europe	9-2-(5)
Bellis perennis	lawn daisy	79	Asteraceae	Europe to W. Asia	9-3-(8)
Berberis darwinii	Darwin's barberry	**162**	Berberidaceae	S. Chile, Patagonia	7-2-(6)
Berberis glaucocarpa	barberry	**162**	Berberidaceae	W. Himalaya	10-12
Blackstonia perfoliata	yellow wort	**113**	Gentianaceae	Europe, S.W. Asia, N. Africa	11-2
Blechnum minus	swamp kiokio fern	**117**	Blechnaceae	N.Z., also Tasmania, Australia	
Bolboschoenus caldwellii	marsh clubrush	**61**	Cyperaceae	N.Z., also Australia	10-2
Bomarea caldasii	bomarea	**67**	Alstroemeriaceae	S. America	10-5-(9)
Borago officinalis	borage	50, **51**	Boraginaceae	C. Europe, Mediterranean	9-5
Brachyglottis bellidioides		**166**	Asteraceae	N.Z.	10-3
Brachyglottis rotundifolia	muttonbird scrub	**153**	Asteraceae	N.Z.	1-2
Brassica fruticulosa	airport cabbage	**64**	Brassicaceae	N. Africa	1-12
Brassica oleracea	wild cabbage	**19**	Brassicaceae	W. Europe, Mediterranean	(7)-10-11-(4)
Brassica rapa	wild turnip	**149**	Brassicaceae	Europe	(7)-9-2-(6)
Bromus sterilis	barren brome	**63**	Poaceae	Europe, S.W. Asia	11-1
Bromus tectorum	downy brome	**63**	Poaceae	Mediterranean	11-1
Brugmansia candida	angel's trumpet	**84**	Solanaceae	Peru, Colombia	1-12

Botanical names	Common names	Page	Family	Place of origin	Flowering months
Buddleja davidii	buddleia	**110**	Buddlejaceae	China	12-2-(4)
Bulbinella hookeri	Maori onion	**41, 42**	Asphodelaceae	N.Z.	11-1
Bulbinella rossii		164	Asphodelaceae	N.Z. subantarctic	11-1

C

Botanical names	Common names	Page	Family	Place of origin	Flowering months
Calendula officinalis	marigold	**30**	Asteraceae	origin unknown	10-5
Calluna vulgaris	heather	**73, 75**	Ericaceae	Europe, Asia Minor, N. Africa	12-3
Calystegia silvativa	convolvulus	**69**	Convolvulaceae	S. Europe	10-5
Calystegia soldanella	shore bindweed	**110, 111**	Convolvulaceae	N.Z., also N. & S. temperate	10-4
Calystegia tuguriorum	native bindweed	**69**	Convolvulaceae	N.Z., also S. America	(9)-11-3
Canna indica	Indian shot	**94**	Cannaceae	West Indies, C. & S. America	11-4
Carex maorica		**117**	Cyperaceae	N.Z.	9-3
Carex pumila	sand sedge	**61**	Cyperaceae	N.Z., also Australia, to China, Japan	11-12
Carmichaelia grandiflora	native broom	**146**	Fabaceae	N.Z.	1-2
Carpobrotus aequilaterus	ice plant	**21**	Aizoaceae	California, Chile	8-1-(5)
Carpobrotus edulis	pig face	**21**	Aizoaceae	S. Africa	(7)-10-2-(6)
Carpobrotus edulis ✕*Disphyma australe*	hybrid ice plant	**21**	Aizoaceae	natural hybrid origin	8-1-(5)
Cedronella canariensis	balm of Gilead	**154**	Lamiaceae	Canary Is., Madeira	11-12-(6)
Celmisia dallii	Dall's daisy	**42**	Asteraceae	N.Z.	12-1
Celmisia gracilenta	grassland daisy	**75**	Asteraceae	N.Z.	10-4
Celmisia lyallii	false spaniard	**166**	Asteraceae	N.Z.	12-2
Celmisia semicordata	mountain daisy	**40**	Asteraceae	N.Z.	12-2
Celmisia traversii		**40**	Asteraceae	N.Z.	12-2
Centranthus ruber	spur valerian	**65, 66, 93**	Valerianaceae	S.W. Europe, Mediterranean	10-6
Centrolepis pallida	pale pincushion	**143**	Centrolepidaceae	N.Z.	11-1
Chamaecytisus palmensis	tree lucerne	**103**	Fabaceae	La Palma, Canary Is.	(3)-4-10
Cheiranthus cheiri	wallflower	**22**	Brassicaceae	Greece, Aegean Is.	7-12-(6)
Chionochloa antarctica	subantarctic snow-tussock	**164**	Poaceae	N.Z. subantarctic	12-1
Chionochloa rubra	red tussock	**42, 75**	Poaceae	N.Z.	12-1
Chrysanthemoides monilifera	bone-seed	**30, 65**	Asteraceae	S. Africa	9-2-(5)
Chrysanthemum segetum	corn marigold	**126**	Asteraceae	Europe, N. Africa, Caucasia	1-12
Cichorium intybus	chicory	**28**	Asteraceae	Europe, W. Asia, N. Africa	(10)-12-4
Clematis foetida		**72**	Ranunculaceae	N.Z.	9-11
Clematis paniculata	puawhaananga	**72, 163**	Ranunculaceae	N.Z.	8-11
Clematis vitalba	old man's beard	**67**	Ranunculaceae	Europe, S.W. Asia	12-5
Clinopodium vulgare	wild basil	**45**	Lamiaceae	Europe, W. Asia, N. America	12-5
Collomia cavanillesii	collomia	**135**	Polemoniaceae	Chile, Argentina	11-4
Colocasia esculenta	taro	**100**	Araceae	S.E. Asia	2-4
Conium maculatum	hemlock	**34, 131**	Apiaceae	Europe, Asia, N. Africa	9-5
Coprosma foetidissima	stinkwood	119, **121**, 153	Rubiaceae	N.Z.	10-11
Coprosma lucida	shining karamu	**153**	Rubiaceae	N.Z.	8-12
Coprosma repens	taupata	**65**	Rubiaceae	N.Z.	9-3
Cordyline australis	ti, cabbage tree	**159**	Asteliaceae	N.Z.	10-1
Coriaria sarmentosa	tutu	**146**	Coriariaceae	N.Z.	10-11-(2)
Corybas macranthus	spider orchid	**158**	Orchidaceae	N.Z.	10-1
Cotoneaster glaucophyllus	cotoneaster	**113**	Rosaceae	China	10-1
Cotula coronopifolia	bachelor's button	**59**	Asteraceae	N.Z., also Australia, Africa, S. America	1-12
Cotyledon orbiculata	pig's ear	**76**	Crassulaceae	S. Africa	12-6
Crataegus monogyna	hawthorn	**169**	Rosaceae	Europe	10-11-(12)
Crepis capillaris	hawksbeard	**31**	Asteraceae	Europe	(7)-9-5-(6)
Crocosmia ✕*crocosmiiflora*	montbretia	**81, 145**	Iridaceae	S. Africa, cult. hybrid	12-4
Cymbalaria muralis	ivy-leaved toadflax	**79**	Scrophulariaceae	S. Europe	10-2
Cynosurus echinatus	rough dogstail	**63**	Poaceae	Mediterranean	12-2

Botanical names	Common names	Page	Family	Place of origin	Flowering months
Cyperus congestus	purple umbrella sedge	118	Cyperaceae	S. Africa	1-12
Cyperus eragrostis	umbrella sedge	118	Cyperaceae	N. & S. America	1-12
Cyperus ustulatus	toetoe upoko-tangata	118	Cyperaceae	N.Z.	11-2
Cytisus scoparius	broom	102, 103	Fabaceae	Europe, Asia Minor, Russia	8-12-(7)

D

Dacrydium cupressinum	rimu	153	Podocarpaceae	N.Z.	
Dactylis glomerata	cocksfoot	23	Poaceae	Europe, N. Africa, temperate Asia	10-4
Daphne laureola		11	Thymelaeaceae	S.W. Europe, N. Africa	5-9
Datura stramonium	thornapple	84	Solanaceae	tropical & subtropical America	11-4
Daucus carota	wild carrot	6, 81, 90	Apiaceae	Europe, Asia, N. Africa	8-5
Dendrobium cunninghamii	lady's slipper orchid	155, 158	Orchidaceae	N.Z.	10-2
Desmoschoenus spiralis	pingao	55	Cyperaceae	N.Z.	11-12
Dianthus plumarius	pink	35	Caryophyllaceae	Europe	10-1-(3)
Digitalis purpurea	foxglove	12	Scrophulariaceae	W. Europe	10-2
Diplotaxis muralis	wall rocket	111	Brassicaceae	C. & S. Europe, N.W. Africa	(7)-10-5-(6)
Dipogon lignosus	mile-a-minute	65, 78	Fabaceae	S. Africa	7-1
Dipsacus sylvestris	wild teasel	169	Dipsacaceae	Europe, to Ukraine, Iran	10-4
Discaria toumatou	matagouri	37	Rhamnaceae	N.Z.	10-1
Disphyma australe	native ice plant	21	Aizoaceae	N.Z.	8-1-(7)
Disphyma clavellatum	Australian ice plant	18, 21	Aizoaceae	Australia	11-1
Dracophyllum longifolium	inaka	153	Epacridaceae	N.Z.	11-1
Dracunculus vulgaris	stink lily	98	Araceae	S. Europe	12
Drosanthemum floribundum		20	Aizoaceae	S. Africa	11-1
Duchesnea indica	Indian strawberry	126	Rosaceae	India, E. Asia	10-7

E

Earina autumnalis	Easter orchid, raupeka	157	Orchidaceae	N.Z.	2-4-(5)
Echium candicans	pride of Madeira	19	Boraginaceae	Macaronesia	(1)-5-11-(12)
Echium pininana	giant bugloss	11	Boraginaceae	Canary Is.	10-2
Echium plantagineum	Paterson's curse	88	Boraginaceae	Mediterranean to S. England	(9)-12-2-(5)
Echium vulgare	viper's bugloss	62, 87, 130	Boraginaceae	Europe, Asia Minor	(10)-11-1-(5)
Eleocharis sphacelata	bamboo spike-sedge	124	Cyperaceae	N.Z., also Australia, PNG	12-2
Epilobium ciliatum	willowherb	117	Onagraceae	N. America	11-3
Erica cinerea	bell heather	75	Ericaceae	W. Europe	12-2
Erica lusitanica	Spanish heath	73	Ericaceae	S.W. Europe	3-12
Erigeron karvinskianus	Mexican daisy	26, 66, 113	Asteraceae	Mexico	9-5-(8)
Escallonia rubra	red escallonia	154	Escalloniaceae	Chile	10-12-(5)
Eschscholzia californica	Californian poppy	37, 130	Papaveraceae	W. USA	(9)-10-4-(6)
Eucalyptus globulus	Tasmanian bluegum	154	Myrtaceae	Tasmania	(8)-10-1
Euphrasia zelandica	eyebright	166	Scrophulariaceae	N.Z.	10-4

F

Foeniculum vulgare	fennel	33, 34, 81	Apiaceae	S. & S.W. Europe	11-5
Fragaria ×ananassa	strawberry	167	Rosaceae	cultivated hybrid	11-4
Fuchsia excorticata	tree fuchsia	159	Onagraceae	N.Z.	6-1-(7)

G

Galega officinalis	goat's rue	104	Fabaceae	Europe, Asia Minor, C. & S. Russia, W. Asia	12-5
Galeobdolon luteum	aluminium plant	46	Lamiaceae	Europe, W. Asia	12-5
Gentiana amabilis		115	Gentianaceae	N.Z.	1-3
Gentiana cerina	gentian	165	Gentianaceae	N.Z.	1-3
Gentiana saxosa	shore gentian	147	Gentianaceae	N.Z.	1-5
Gentiana corymbifera		166	Gentianaceae	N.Z.	12-3
Gladiolus ×hortulanus	parrot gladiolus	96	Iridaceae	Africa, Arabia	10-12

Botanical names	Common names	Page	Family	Place of origin	Flowering months
Glaucium flavum	horned poppy	**111**	Papaveraceae	W. Europe, Mediterranean, S.W. Asia	11-3
Glechoma hederacea	ground ivy	**46**	Lamiaceae	temperate Eurasia	9-5
Glossostigma elatinoides	flicks	**142**	Scrophulariaceae	N.Z., also Australia	10-4
Gomphocarpus fruticosus	swan plant	70	Asclepiadaceae	Southern Africa	12-5
Gratiola sexdentata	shorebright	**143**	Scrophulariaceae	N.Z.	10-4
Griselinia littoralis	broadleaf	**153**	Griseliniaceae	N.Z.	10-12

H

Hebe elliptica	shore koromiko	**147**	Scrophulariaceae	N.Z., also southern S. America, Falkland Is.	11-2
Hebe hectorii	a whipcord hebe	**166**	Scrophulariaceae	N.Z.	12-2
Hebe salicifolia	willow-leaved koromiko	**146**	Scrophulariaceae	N.Z.	12-4
Hebe topiaria		**42, 43**	Scrophulariaceae	N.Z.	(11)-1-(4)
Hectorella caespitosa		**41**	Hectorellaceae	N.Z.	1-2
Hedychium flavescens	yellow ginger	**97**	Zingiberaceae	Madagascar, India	(1)-2-6
Hedychium gardnerianum	Kahili ginger	**81, 97**	Zingiberaceae	India, Himalaya	(1)-2-3
Helianthus annuus	sunflower	**149**	Asteraceae	N. America	1-3
Helichrysum intermedium	whipcord daisy	12, **13**	Asteraceae	N.Z.	11-1
Heracleum mantegazzianum	giant hogweed	34	Apiaceae	S.W. Asia	12-2
Heracleum sphondylium	cow parsnip	**34**	Apiaceae	Europe, Mediterranean, N.W. Africa, W. & N. Asia	12-2
Hieracium pilosella	mouse-ear hawkweed	36	Asteraceae	Europe, N. & C. Asia	10-2-(5)
Hieracium praealtum	king devil	36, **37**	Asteraceae	Europe	(9)-11-1-(4)
Hoheria lyallii	mountain ribbonwood	**146**	Malvaceae	N.Z.	11-3
Holcus lanatus	Yorkshire fog	**10**	Poaceae	Europe, N.W. Africa, temperate Asia	11-2-(5)
Hordeum vulgare	barley	**62**	Poaceae	Eurasia, cultivated origin	11-1
Hyacinthoides non-scripta	bluebell, scilla	**66**	Hyacinthaceae	Europe	9-11
Hydrangea macrophylla	hydrangea	**125**	Hydrangeaceae	Japan	11-3
Hypericum perforatum	St John's wort	**131, 132**	Clusiaceae	Europe, W. Asia, N. Africa	12-5
Hypochoeris radicata	catsear	**28, 31, 109**	Asteraceae	Europe, N. Africa	11-3-(10)
Hypsela rivalis	bumbles	**142**	Lobeliaceae	N.Z.	11-4

I

Impatiens glandulifera	fireman's helmet, Himalayan balsam, touch-me-not	119, **121**	Balsaminaceae	Himalaya	11-3
Ipomoea batatas	kumara	86	Convolvulaceae	prob. northern S. America	
Ipomoea cairica	railway creeper	**93**	Convolvulaceae	N.Z., also old world tropics	10-5
Ipomoea indica	blue morning glory	**70**	Convolvulaceae	pantropical	1-12
Iris foetidissima	stinking iris	137, **138**	Iridaceae	Europe, N. Africa	11-12
Iris pseudacorus	yellow flag	**137**	Iridaceae	Europe, Asia, N. Africa	11-12
Isolepis nodosa	knobby clubrush	**60**	Cyperaceae	N.Z., also Australia, other S. hemisphere coasts	11-2
Iti lacustris		142	Brassicaceae	N.Z.	8-5

J

Jasminum polyanthum	jasmine	70, **71**	Oleaceae	W. China	1-12
Juncus kraussii var. *australiensis*	sea rush	**61**	Juncaceae	N.Z., also Australia	11-2

K

Kniphofia uvaria	red hot poker	**136**	Asphodelaceae	S. Africa	1-3
Kunzea ericoides	kanuka	**12, 16**	Myrtaceae	N.Z.	(9)-11-2

L

Lagurus ovatus	harestail	**60**	Poaceae	S. Europe	11-3
Lamium album	white dead nettle	**44**	Lamiaceae	temperate Eurasia	9-12-(8)

Botanical names	Common names	Page	Family	Place of origin	Flowering months
Lampranthus spectabilis		**20**	Aizoaceae	S. Africa	9-2
Lantana camara	lantana	**87**	Verbenaceae	tropical America	1-12
Lathyrus latifolius	everlasting pea	**101**	Fabaceae	C. & S. Europe	(9)-11-2-(5)
Lathyrus tingitanus	Tangier pea	**65**	Fabaceae	Mediterranean	8-5
Lavatera arborea	tree mallow	**119**	Malvaceae	W.& S. Europe, N. Africa	8-5
Lepidium oleraceum	Cook's scurvy grass	**58**	Brassicaceae	N.Z.	(7)-12-2-(6)
Leptocarpus similis	oioi	**59**	Restionaceae	N.Z.	10-12
Leptospermum scoparium	manuka, tea-tree	**16, 42, 74, 75, 163**	Myrtaceae	N.Z., also Australia, Tasmania	11-2-(10)
Leucanthemum vulgare	oxeye daisy	**31, 81**	Asteraceae	temperate Eurasia	(8)-10-2-(5)
Leucogenes grandiceps	South Island edelweiss	**41**	Asteraceae	N.Z.	12-3
Leucojum aestivum	snowflake	**23, 24**	Amaryllidaceae	C. & S. Europe	7-10
Leycesteria formosa	Himalayan honeysuckle	**27**	Caprifoliaceae	temperate Himalaya	12-5
Ligustrum lucidum	tree privet	**95**	Oleaceae	China	11-3
Lilium formosanum	lily	**92**	Liliaceae	Taiwan	(1)-2-4
Linaria genistifolia		**134**	Scrophulariaceae	Europe, W. & S.W. Asia	1-3
Linaria purpurea	purple linaria	**33, 131, 134**	Scrophulariaceae	Italy	1-12
Linaria vulgaris	toadflax	**134**	Scrophulariaceae	Europe, W. Asia	11-3
Linum bienne	pale flax	**113**	Linaceae	W. Europe, Mediterranean to Caucasia, Iraq, Iran	11-4
Linum monogynum	native linen flax	**15**	Linaceae	N.Z.	9-3
Linum usitatissimum	linseed	15	Linaceae	origin uncertain, prob. Europe	10-4
Lolium perenne	perennial ryegrass	32	Poaceae	Europe, temperate Asia, N. Africa	11-3
Lonicera japonica	Japanese honeysuckle	**71**	Caprifoliaceae	E. Asia	9-5
Lonicera periclymenum	English honeysuckle	**154**	Caprifoliaceae	Europe, N. Africa	12-8
Lotus pedunculatus	lotus	**10, 104**	Fabaceae	Europe, N. Africa, Asia	12-3
Ludwigia peploides subsp. *montevidensis*	primrose willow	**114**	Onagraceae	tropical & subtropical America	11-2
Lunaria annua	honesty	**26, 27, 169**	Brassicaceae	S.E. Europe	(9)-10-11-(3)
Lupinus arboreus	tree lupin	**56, 57**	Fabaceae	California	10-4-(6)
Lupinus polyphyllus	Russell lupin	**36**	Fabaceae	western N. America	(9)-11-2-(5)
Luzuriaga parviflora	lantern-berry, nohi	**151**	Luzuriagaceae	N.Z.	12-3
Lychnis coronaria	rose campion	**131**	Caryophyllaceae	Europe, N.W. Africa, Asia Minor	(8)-12-2-(6)
Lycium ferocissimum	boxthorn	**85**	Solanaceae	S. Africa	7-3

M

Malva sylvestris	large-flowered mallow	**130**	Malvaceae	Europe, N. Africa, S.W. Asia	11-5
Medicago lupulina	black medick	**105**	Fabaceae	S. Europe to W. Asia, N. Africa	10-5
Medicago sativa	lucerne, alfalfa	**6**	Fabaceae	Mediterranean, W. Asia	11-3-(5)
Melianthus major	Cape honey flower	**148, 149**	Melianthaceae	S. Africa	7-4
Melilotus albus	sweet clover	**6**	Fabaceae	Europe, Asia	(9)-11-5-(8)
Mentha pulegium	pennyroyal	**45**	Lamiaceae	Europe, N. Africa, Macaronesia	11-5
Mentha spicata	spearmint	**52**	Lamiaceae	Europe (cultivated origin)	1-5
Metrosideros excelsa	pohutukawa	**106, 163**	Myrtaceae	N.Z.	12-1
Metrosideros fulgens	scarlet rata vine	**107**	Myrtaceae	N.Z.	2-6
Metrosideros perforata	mat rata	**106**	Myrtaceae	N.Z.	1-3
Metrosideros robusta	northern rata	**107**	Myrtaceae	N.Z.	11-1
Metrosideros umbellata	southern rata	**107, 108, 153, 165**	Myrtaceae	N.Z.	11-2-(10)
Microtis unifolia	onion orchid	**156**	Orchidaceae	N.Z., also Australia	11-3
Mimulus guttatus	monkey musk	115, **116**	Scrophulariaceae	western N. America	11-3
Mimulus moschatus	musk	**116**	Scrophulariaceae	western N. America	(7)-12-3-(6)
Mimulus repens		115, **116**	Scrophulariaceae	N.Z.	10-3

Table 177

Botanical names	Common names	Page	Family	Place of origin	Flowering months
Muscari armeniacum	grape hyacinth, match heads	24	Hyacinthaceae	Asia Minor	8-10
Myoporum insulare	boobialla	56	Myoporaceae	Australia, Lord Howe I.	9-6
Myoporum laetum	ngaio	56	Myoporaceae	N.Z.	(7)-11-1-(4)
Myosotis rakiura	Stewart Island forget-me-not	150, **151**	Boraginaceae	N.Z.	10-2
Myosotis sylvatica	forget-me-not	24	Boraginaceae	temperate Eurasia	3-11
Myriophyllum aquaticum	parrot's feather	114	Haloragaceae	S. America	9-2
Myriophyllum votschii	mini-milfoil	143	Haloragaceae	N.Z.	11-2

N

Narcissus pseudonarcissus	daffodil	24	Amaryllidaceae	Spain, France	8-10
Nassella trichotoma	nassella tussock	63	Poaceae	S. America	10-11-(9)
Navarretia squarrosa	Californian stinkweed	135	Polemoniaceae	western N. America	11-4
Neopaxia australasica	pink boys	142	Portulacaceae	N.Z., also Tasmania, Australia	11-3

O

Oenanthe pimpinelloides	parsley dropwort	90	Apiaceae	Europe, Asia Minor	10-4
Oenothera glazioviana	evening primrose	**92, 110**	Onagraceae	Europe (cultivated origin)	12-4
Oenothera stricta	sand primrose	**6, 111**	Onagraceae	southern S. America	11-6
Olearia ilicifolia	mountain holly	146	Asteraceae	N.Z.	11-1
Olearia oporina	teteaweka	147, 150	Asteraceae	N.Z.	11-12-(3)
Onopordum acanthium	cotton thistle	119, **120**	Asteraceae	Europe, W. & C. Asia	12-2
Origanum vulgare	wild marjoram	133	Lamiaceae	Europe, W. Asia	12-4
Oxalis pes-caprae	Bermuda buttercup	80	Oxalidaceae	South Africa	1-12
Ozothamnus leptophyllus	cottonwood	42	Asteraceae	N.Z.	11-3

P

Pachystegia insignis	Marlborough rock daisy	50	Asteraceae	N.Z.	12-2
Papaver dubium	long-headed poppy	134	Papaveraceae	Europe, Asia	10-2
Papaver rhoeas	field poppy	134	Papaveraceae	temperate Eurasia, N.W. Africa	(10)-12-1-(4)
Parahebe catarractae		164	Scrophulariaceae	N.Z.	11-6
Parentucellia viscosa	tarweed	117	Scrophulariaceae	W. Europe, Mediterranean, Macaronesia	11-5
Parochetus communis	shamrock pea	127	Fabaceae	E. Africa, Asia	10-4-(9)
Passiflora mollissima	banana passionfruit	69	Passifloraceae	northern S. America	1-12
Pastinaca sativa	parsnip	34	Apiaceae	Europe	(10)-1-3-(5)
Pelargonium ✕ hortorum	zonal pelargonium	37	Geraniaceae	cultivated hybrid	1-12
Pelargonium peltatum	ivy-leaved geranium	37	Geraniaceae	South Africa	1-12
Peraxilla colensoi	red mistletoe	144	Loranthaceae	N.Z.	11-2
Petasites fragrans	winter heliotrope	22	Asteraceae	N. Africa	6-9
Petroselinum crispum	parsley	52	Apiaceae	Europe	10-5
Phormium cookianum	mountain flax	15, 16	Phormiaceae	N.Z.	11-1
Phormium tenax	harakeke, flax	13, 14	Phormiaceae	N.Z., also Norfolk I.	11-1
Phyllachne colensoi		41	Stylidiaceae	N.Z., also Tasmania	12-3
Physalis peruviana	cape gooseberry	85	Solanaceae	tropical S. America	1-12
Phytolacca octandra	inkweed	89	Phytolaccaceae	mountains of tropical S. & C. America	11-8
Pimelea gnidia		147	Thymelaeaceae	N.Z.	10-3
Pittosporum eugenioides	lemonwood, tarata	160	Pittosporaceae	N.Z.	10-12
Pittosporum tenuifolium	kohuhu	160	Pittosporaceae	N.Z.	9-12
Pleurophyllum criniferum		**164,** 165	Asteraceae	N.Z. subantarctic	12-2
Pleurophyllum speciosum		164	Asteraceae	N.Z. subantarctic	12-2
Polygonum capitatum	pink-head knotweed	80	Polygonaceae	warm temperate Himalaya	1-12
Polygonum persicaria	willow weed	149	Polygonaceae	temperate N. hemisphere	1-12
Polypogon monspeliensis	beard grass	61	Poaceae	Eurasia	12-3
Pomaderris apetala	tainui	154	Rhamnaceae	N.Z., also S.E. Australia, Tasmania	11-2

Botanical names	Common names	Page	Family	Place of origin	Flowering months
Potamogeton cheesemanii	pondweed	**114**	Potamogetonaceae	N.Z., also Australia	11-2
Prunella vulgaris	selfheal	**117**	Lamiaceae	N. temperate	11-4-(10)
Prunus ✕ domestica	plum	**24, 168**	Rosaceae	cultivated hybrid	8-10
Psychrophila obtusa	white caltha	**39**	Ranunculaceae	N.Z.	10-12
Pteridium esculentum	bracken	**10, 75**	Pteridaceae	N.Z., also Australia, Pacific	
Pterostylis banksii	greenhood orchid	**156**	Orchidaceae	N.Z.	10-1

R

Ranunculus buchananii	a mountain buttercup	**38,** 40	Ranunculaceae	N.Z.	12-2
Ranunculus flammula	spearwort	140, **141**	Ranunculaceae	Europe, Caucasus, N.W. Africa	10-3-(6)
Ranunculus lyallii	Mount Cook lily	**38,** 39	Ranunculaceae	N.Z.	10-1
Ranunculus sericophyllus	yellow mountain buttercup	**39,** 40	Ranunculaceae	N.Z.	12-1
Raoulia youngii		**41**	Asteraceae	N.Z.	12-2
Rhododendron ponticum	rhododendron	**25**	Ericaceae	S.E. Europe, Asia Minor	10-12
Rhopalostylis sapida	nikau	**161**	Arecaceae	N.Z.	11-4
Ribes sanguineum	flowering currant	**24, 27**	Grossulariaceae	western N. America	7-10-(3)
Ribes uva-crispa	gooseberry	**167**	Grossulariaceae	Europe, N. Africa	8-11
Rorippa microphylla	watercress	**52**	Brassicaceae	Europe	(8)-11-4-(6)
Rosa canina	dog rose	**49**	Rosaceae	Europe, S.W. Africa	10-1
Rosa rubiginosa	sweet brier	**9, 47, 63**	Rosaceae	Europe, N. Africa	11-1
Rosa wichuraiana cv. 'Alberic Barbier'		25, **49**	Rosaceae	cultivated hybrid	10-4
Rubus cissoides	bush lawyer	**72**	Rosaceae	N.Z.	8-12
Rubus fruticosus agg.	blackberry	**48, 167**	Rosaceae	N. temperate	10-4
Rubus idaeus	raspberry	**167**	Rosaceae	N. temperate, E. Asia	11-1
Rubus phoenicolasius	Japanese wineberry	**47**	Rosaceae	E. Asia	11-1
Rumex acetosella	sheep's sorrel	**10**	Polygonaceae	Europe	(7)-10-3-(6)
Rumex crispus	curled dock	**34, 169**	Polygonaceae	Europe, N. Africa, W. Asia	11-4

S

Salix ✕ reichardtii	pussy willow	**24**	Salicaceae	origin unknown	8-10
Sambucus nigra	elder	**168**	Caprifoliaceae	Europe, W. Asia, N. Africa	11-12-(1)
Schizostylis coccinea	Kaffir lily	**138**	Iridaceae	S. Africa	3-5
Sedum acre	stonecrop	**129**	Crassulaceae	Europe, N. Africa, W. Asia	11-3
Sedum praealtum	shrubby stonecrop	**19**	Crassulaceae	Mexico	(7)-9-11-(5)
Selliera radicans	selliera	**142**	Goodeniaceae	N.Z., also Tasmania, Australia, Chile	12-3
Senecio elegans	purple groundsel	**57**	Asteraceae	South Africa	8-5
Senecio jacobaea	ragwort	**30, 31**	Asteraceae	Europe, W. Asia	11-4-(7)
Senecio minimus	fireweed	**31**	Asteraceae	N.Z., also Aust., W. USA	10-4
Senecio skirrhodon	gravel groundsel	**80**	Asteraceae	Madagascar, Mozambique to South Africa	12-1
Silene gallica	catchfly	**63**	Caryophyllaceae	Europe	(7)-10-2-(6)
Silene latifolia	white campion	**65**	Caryophyllaceae	Europe, N.W. Africa, S.W. Asia	(9)-11-3-(6)
Silybum marianum	variegated thistle	119, **120**	Asteraceae	Mediterranean, S.W. Europe	11-1-(2)
Simplicia laxa		**128**	Poaceae	N.Z.	11-3
Sisyrinchium "blue"		136, **137**	Iridaceae	? America	11-12
Solanum americanum	small-flowered nightshade	**82**	Solanaceae	N.Z., also America, Africa, S.E. Asia, Pacific	1-12
Solanum dulcamara	bittersweet	**168**	Solanaceae	Eurasia, N. Africa	11-3
Solanum laciniatum	poroporo	**57, 86**	Solanaceae	N.Z., also S.E. Australia, Tasmania	10-5-(9)
Solanum linnaeanum	apple of Sodom	**83**	Solanaceae	northern Africa	9-5
Solanum marginatun	white-edged nightshade	**83**	Solanaceae	prob. N.E. Africa	11-3
Solanum mauritianum	woolly nightshade	**82**	Solanaceae	S. Brazil, Uruguay	1-12

Table **179**

Botanical names	Common names	Page	Family	Place of origin	Flowering months
Solanum tuberosum	potato	**86**	Solanaceae	Andes	11-4
Sonchus kirkii	puha	53	Asteraceae	N.Z.	11-4
Sonchus oleraceus	sow thistle, puha	**52, 57, 60**	Asteraceae	Europe, N. Africa, N.& W. Asia	(8)-11-4-(5)
Sophora microphylla	kowhai	**12, 163**	Fabaceae	N.Z., also southern S. America	(7)-8-10
Sorbus aucuparia	rowan	**168**	Rosaceae	Eurasia	10-11
Sparaxis tricolor	harlequin flower	**66**	Iridaceae	South Africa	9-10
Spartium junceum	Spanish broom	**103**	Fabaceae	Mediterranean	8-5
Spinifex sericeus	spinifex	**60**	Poaceae	N.Z.	11-2
Stachys sylvatica	hedge woundwort	**44**	Lamiaceae	temperate Eurasia	9-5

T

Taraxacum officinale	dandelion	**29**	Asteraceae	Europe	(7)-9-11-(6)
Taxus baccata	yew	**43**	Taxaceae	Europe, N. Africa, W. Asia to Himalaya	
Tecomaria capensis	Cape honeysuckle	**71**	Bignoniaceae	South Africa	1-12
Teline monspessulana	Montpellier broom	**103**	Fabaceae	Mediterranean, Asia Minor, Azores	5-11-(4)
Teline stenopetala		**103**	Fabaceae	Canary Is.	7-4
Thymus vulgaris	thyme	**130**	Lamiaceae	Medit.	9-12-(1)
Tradescantia fluminensis	wandering Jew	**123**	Commelinaceae	S. America	1-12
Tragopogon porrifolius	salsify	**61**	Asteraceae	Mediterranean	(9)-12-2-(3)
Trifolium arvense	haresfoot trefoil	**105, 111**	Fabaceae	Europe, Asia Minor, Caucasia, N. & W. Asia, N. Africa	(8)-12-3-(5)
Trifolium fragiferum	strawberry clover	**61**	Fabaceae	Europe to W. Asia, N. Africa	11-5
Trifolium hybridum	alsike clover	**105**	Fabaceae	S. Europe to Caucasia	11-3
Trifolium pratense	red clover	**6, 105**	Fabaceae	Europe to W. Asia, N. Africa	10-3-(5)
Trifolium repens	white clover	**10**, 32, **105**	Fabaceae	Europe, N. & W. Asia, N. Africa	7-3
Trifolium tomentosum	woolly clover	**104**	Fabaceae	Mediterranean to W. Asia	10-2
Tripleurospermum inodorum	scentless mayweed	**6, 149**	Asteraceae	Mediterranean to W. Asia, S. Russia	(8)-1-2-(5)
Tropaeolum majus	garden nasturtium	**91**	Tropaeolaceae	N. Andes	(1)-9-5-(12)
Tropaeolum speciosum	Chilean flame creeper	**68**	Tropaeolaceae	Chile	11-4
Tussilago farfara	coltsfoot	**29**	Asteraceae	Europe, N. Africa, N.& W. Asia	10
Typha orientalis	raupo	**117**	Typhaceae	N.Z., also to Australia, Philippines	12-1

U

Ulex europaeus	gorse	**2, 32, 103**	Fabaceae	W. Europe to Italy	9-11-(8)
Utricularia novae-zelandiae	bladderwort	**143**	Lentibulariaceae	N.Z.	11-3

V

Verbascum thapsus	woolly mullein	**6, 128**	Scrophulariaceae	Europe, W. Asia	(10)-12-3-(5)
Verbena bonariensis	purple-top	**81, 93**	Verbenaceae	eastern S. America	12-6
Vinca major	periwinkle	**66**	Apocynaceae	Mediterranean	1-12

W

Wahlenbergia albomarginata	harebell	**75**, 132, **133**	Campanulaceae	N.Z.	11-3
Watsonia bulbillifera	watsonia	**94**, 95	Iridaceae	S. Africa	10-12
Weinmannia racemosa	kamahi	**108, 153**	Cunoniaceae	N.Z.	10-12-(9)

Z

Zantedeschia aethiopica	arum lily, calla lily	**66, 99**	Araceae	S. Africa	(7)-10-12-(4)

Index

Page numbers in **bold** indicate pictorial reference; plain numbers are text reference only.